ISRAEL AND THE LAST DAYS

APPLYING RULES OF INTERPRETATION TO END-TIME PROPHECY

Kree Foster

WestBow
PRESS
A DIVISION OF THOMAS NELSON

WestBow Press books may be ordered through booksellers or by contacting:

WestBow Press
A Division of Thomas Nelson
1663 Liberty Drive
Bloomington, IN 47403
www.westbowpress.com
1-(866) 928-1240

Because of the dynamic nature of the Internet, any web addresses or links contained in this book may have changed since publication and may no longer be valid. The views expressed in this work are solely those of the author and do not necessarily reflect the views of the publisher, and the publisher hereby disclaims any responsibility for them.

Any people depicted in stock imagery provided by Thinkstock are models, and such images are being used for illustrative purposes only.

Certain stock imagery © Thinkstock.

ISBN: 978-1-4497-5556-0 (sc)
ISBN: 978-1-4497-5555-3 (hc)
ISBN: 978-1-4497-5557-7 (e)

Library of Congress Control Number: 2012910190

Printed in the United States of America

WestBow Press rev. date: 07/05/2012

CONTENTS

DEDICATION

I DEDICATE THIS BOOK TO my beautiful wife, Jennifer. I am eternally grateful for her love and support, which propels me in the pursuit of God and his will. Jennifer, you are the love of my life. Thank you for being such a great mom to our two beautiful girls, Ariel and Sadie. Thank you for being there for me even when things are so busy and hectic.

I love you!
-Kree

INTRODUCTION
Israel and the Last Days

As a teen, I attended a Baptist Church. It was a great church, but during that time I didn't pursue truth very aggressively. Frankly, it wasn't very important to me. Then, at the age of 20, I got serious with Jesus. I began to pattern my life after the Lord and attend church as much as possible. Soon afterward, an important truth became very evident to me: people have many different opinions on Scripture. I asked a lot of questions back then (and I still do). I asked questions in Sunday school, and because I love to do research, I continued to ask others the same questions. Then, I compared the answers. Furthermore, I realized that different denominations had different interpretations as well. I began to wonder, who is right? How do you know if your doctrine is what God says? The only reason we have different denominations is because there are different beliefs. Who is right? I mean, someone has to be right. My thoughts at the time and still today are that this should not be this way. The church of Jesus Christ should be able to agree on truth. As I continued looking into this, I discovered that the church began to spiral downward after the first century. The doctrines that Jesus taught began to wither away over time. Eventually, the Catholic Church arose, and many teachings of the Scripture were perverted. One of the things that had a great impact on the believers during that time was the fact that the Scriptures were hidden from common, ordinary folks. The Catholic Church believed that only ministers could understand and interpret the Scripture. However, the truth is that the devil wanted to keep the Word of God hidden from the believers. Satan is afraid of the Word of God—if he could take the Word away from believers, he could remove their power to resist him. This practice continued for years. Yet another belief of the time was that the Holy Scriptures should only be written in Latin. This also kept the common folks from reading it because the Scripture was not available in their own language. People fought against this belief, and many great men of God began to defy the Catholic Church and translate the Scriptures into other languages. Many of those people died for doing so. God desired to restore his church and his doctrines. This could not be achieved until the Word of God was made available to the public. Satan fought to keep it hidden, but he failed. God's people rose up in the face of death and did what they believed God was calling them to do. When people received the Scriptures in their own languages, the grip of the Catholic Church began to be weakened. Martin Luther, one of the great religious pioneers, found a personal conviction when he read, "The just shall live by faith." The house of cards that had been constructed began to fall. Since then, God has restored many more truths that had been hidden from the body of Christ. Thank God we have the Scriptures in our own language! Still today, there are many different opinions on these subjects. It was this fact that led me to work toward interpreting Scripture in such a way that absolutely nails it down and dispels all the different opinions in order to present the truth of the Word of God. In this book, I pray you will also take the principles of interpretation and apply them to restoring the much needed truth of the Word of God. All God needs is someone who is available. Are you available?

FOREWORD

I COUNT IT A GREAT honor to write these words as a foreword to this exciting book by my good friend and brother in Christ, Kree Foster. I have been greatly inspired and encouraged through the insights I have received from the Lord through this great man of God. I believe that this book is a strategic revelation for the day in which we are living.

There is a lot of information today that is circulating throughout the Body of Christ on the subject of the end times. With so many different views, it can be confusing to know exactly what to believe about the second coming of Christ. Over one third of the Bible is made up of prophecy. If this much of the Bible contains prophecy, then it is imperative that we rightly divide the word of truth and have a proper understanding of prophecy.

The best way to understand the Word of God is to follow the rules of biblical interpretation, allowing the Word of God to interpret itself. "No prophecy of the Scripture is of any private interpretation" (2 Peter 1:20). If you don't follow the rules of biblical interpretation, it can become very easy to get off track and make the Bible say something very different than what is actually being said. That is the reason why there are so many different denominations in the Body of Christ, and the reason why there are so many different views regarding the end times. In this book, you will discover that Kree has done a masterful job of rightly dividing the word of truth. It is refreshing to hear the teaching that is contained within this book. It is effective, biblical, and accurate. I believe Kree has hit the bull's eye and has revealed the real truth about the end times.

In this book, you will find that in order to properly understand the truth about the end times, you must recognize the harmony between the words of Jesus and His completion and fulfillment of all that the Old Testament prophets said. There are many Christians today who have a mentality that says, "I just hope the Lord comes soon and raptures me out of this old world and takes me away from all of my problems." Many of the end time teachings that are popular today would make you think that Jesus is coming back for a weak, defeated, beat up bride hiding in a hole somewhere. The Bible makes it clear that He is coming back for an overcoming church that is triumphant over all of the works of the devil, and radiant with the glory of God.

You will be greatly encouraged as you read this book. It exemplifies the victory of the finished work of Christ and unveils His love and grace. Whatever we learn about the end times should not fill us with fear, but rather it should comfort and edify us, it should impart God's grace and love. That is exactly what this book does as it reveals the truth of God's Word about the end times. It will put you at peace about the future, because that's what the Word communicates: victory, grace, and peace.

May God richly bless you as you read this book!
Evangelist Daniel Adams

Chapter 1

INTERPRETATION!
INTERPRETATION!
INTERPRETATION!

I F YOU HAVE BEEN A Christian for more than a few days, you have
wondered about the end times. What's going to happen? Who is the
Antichrist? How bad is it going to get? If people miss the rapture, what will
happen to them? Strangely, though, for every prophecy teacher you hear,
there is a different opinion on all these various things. It seems that some
teachers change their doctrine every week with the current news of the day.
How can we know what to believe?

First of all, we cannot just accept a person's teaching because that person
studied and *should* know what he or she is talking about, no matter who it
is. Even the best of us can get it wrong. We must study for ourselves and let
God speak His revelation to us personally.

"Of these things put *them* in remembrance, charging *them* before the
Lord that they strive not about words to no profit, *but* to the subverting of
the hearers. Study to shew thyself approved unto God, a workman that
needeth not to be ashamed, *rightly dividing the word of truth*" (2 Tim. 2:14–15
KJV, emphasis mine).

I believe that we must preach truth only. What do I mean? Well, if we
cannot prove a doctrine *absolutely*, then it is speculation. What a shame it

is for a preacher who should be proclaiming truth, to proclaim speculation as truth. If we are commanded by the Word of God to "rightly divide the Word of Truth," then there must be a method to find and confirm truth in the Bible. That is what we are going to discover throughout this book.

When I first began this journey, I had no particular method of interpretation. I just read the Scripture, tried to comprehend it as best I could, and put what I did understand into practice. There is nothing wrong with that, if that is where you are. I did read Scripture quite a bit and did receive some revelation, but there were many different things I didn't understand. I began to ask others' opinions on those things. There were many different opinions, and it seemed as though everyone had a good point or two. How could I know for sure what God thought?

One Sunday morning in church, the pastor was teaching on the book of Revelation. I had read that book many times without much comprehension. As he taught, he looked like he was absolutely sure of what he was saying, but it didn't make sense to me. As it turns out, he was teaching from a commentary and had not questioned those doctrines at all. I was so confused. None of these things made sense to me, and I didn't know what to believe. I came home and sat on my bed, wondering what to do. Then I did the only thing I could—I prayed. Don't get me wrong; it wasn't a grand, super spiritual prayer. I simply spoke to my heavenly Father as if he were standing right in front of me. "Lord, I don't know what to believe. I don't know what is true and what is not; you're going to have to teach me." Then I lay down on my bed in silence. All these thoughts, Scriptures, and questions were still racing through my mind. Finally, I calmed down and was almost asleep, when a Scripture came into my mind. To my surprise, God had given me my first solid lead to the truth of the end times. All this time, the only thing I needed to do was ask.

That short little prayer changed my perspective, and God began to lead my study rather than me fumbling around confused. I discovered that the very first step in "rightly dividing the Word of Truth" was simply to ask God. I wish I could say that all of the revelation came quickly, but it didn't. God had to teach me to think differently about several things, so he could get his points across to me. The revelation came to me a little at a time, here and there. There are still many things I don't understand, but I now know how to ask, seek, knock, and listen for God's direction. Throughout this book, I will take you on a journey that will change how you study Scripture. Consider the concepts in prayer as you go, and let God speak to you. He definitely will.

As I studied the things God began to show me, I discovered that there are specific rules for interpreting Scripture correctly. The major rules of interpretation are context, confirmation, pattern, and type and shadow. Context consists of the following:

+ Who is talking?
+ Who is being spoken to?
+ Where is the location?
+ What is the time period?
+ What are the beliefs of all the people involved?
+ What is the relationship of the people with God?
+ Does the interpretation fit with surrounding verses, chapters, and the Bible as a whole?

Confirmation means building a doctrine upon more than one Scripture. We must have at least two Scriptures to *confirm* something as true.

"Ye judge after the flesh; I judge no man. And yet if I judge, my judgment is true: for I am not alone, but I and the Father that sent me. It is also written in your law, *that the testimony of two men is true*"(John 8:15–17 KJV, emphasis mine).

"One witness shall not rise up against a man for any iniquity, or for any sin, in any sin that he sinneth: *at the mouth of two witnesses, or at the mouth of three witnesses, shall the matter be established*"(Deut. 19:14–15 KJV, emphasis mine).

The spirit of this principle is to establish a truth through more than one source. Take a Scripture and put it on the shelf until the Lord shows a second or third Scripture that clearly says the same thing, and then that belief is established and confirmed. Confirmation is the most violated rule of interpretation. For example:

"They shall take up serpents; and if they drink any deadly thing, it shall not hurt them; they shall lay hands on the sick, and they shall recover"(Mark 16:18 KJV).

According to one interpretation of this Scripture, we are supposed to handle deadly serpents to test our faith. Well, before you head off to go rattlesnake hunting, you might want to find other Scriptures that say the same thing in order establish that belief as truth. Think of how many church splits and doctrinal fights could have been avoided just by applying this one rule.

Next is pattern. Pattern is usually a pattern of numbers with significance, such as *forty*. Forty is a number of temptation and judgment.

"Wherefore as the Holy Ghost saith, Today if ye will hear his voice, Harden not your hearts, as in the provocation, in the day of temptation in the wilderness: When your fathers tempted me, proved me, and saw my works forty years" (Heb. 3:7–9 KJV).

God put numbers in the Bible to guide us toward particular truths. Throughout the forty years the Israelites spent in the wilderness, they questioned God's ability to care for them. Their unbelief occurred in three main areas: protection, food, and worship.

PROTECTION

"And when Pharaoh drew nigh, the children of Israel lifted up their eyes, and, behold, the Egyptians marched after them; and they were sore afraid: and the children of Israel cried out unto the LORD. And they said unto Moses, because *there were* no graves in Egypt, hast thou taken us away to die in the wilderness? Wherefore hast thou dealt thus with us, to carry us forth out of Egypt? *Is* not this the word that we did tell thee in Egypt, saying, Let us alone, that we may serve the Egyptians? For *it had been* better for us to serve the Egyptians, than that *we should die in the wilderness*" (Ex. 14:10–12 KJV, emphasis mine).

FOOD

"And the whole congregation of the children of Israel murmured against Moses and Aaron in the wilderness: And the children of Israel said unto them, Would to God we had died by the hand of the LORD in the land of Egypt, when we sat by the flesh pots, *and* when we did eat bread to the full; for ye have brought us forth into this wilderness, *to kill this whole assembly with hunger"* (Ex. 16:2–3 KJV, emphasis mine).

WORSHIP

"And the LORD said unto Moses, Go, get thee down; for thy people, which thou broughtest out of the land of Egypt, have corrupted *themselves:* They have turned aside quickly out of the way which I commanded them: *they have made them a molten calf, and have worshipped it,* and have sacrificed thereunto, and said, These *be* thy gods, O Israel, which have brought thee up out of the land of Egypt" (Ex. 32:7–8 KJV, emphasis mine).

What does that have to do with anything, you ask? Well, Jesus was tempted for forty days in the wilderness and he was tempted in the same three areas, but he passed the test.

FOOD

"Then was Jesus led up of the Spirit into the wilderness to be tempted of the devil. And when he had fasted forty days and forty nights, he was afterward an hungred. And when the tempter came to him, he said, If thou be the Son of God, *command that these stones be made bread.* But he answered and said, It is written, Man shall not live by bread alone, but by every word that proceedeth out of the mouth of God" (Matt. 10:1–4 KJV, emphasis mine).

PROTECTION

"Then the devil taketh him up into the holy city, and setteth him on a pinnacle of the temple, And saith unto him, If thou be the Son of God, *cast thyself down:* for it is written, He shall give his angels charge concerning thee: and in *their* hands they shall bear thee up, lest at any time thou dash thy foot against a stone. Jesus said unto him, It is written again, Thou shalt not tempt the Lord thy God" (Matt. 10:5–7 KJV, emphasis mine).

Worship

"Again, the devil taketh him up into an exceeding high mountain, and sheweth him all the kingdoms of the world, and the glory of them; And saith unto him, All these things will I give thee, *if thou wilt fall down and worship me*. Then saith Jesus unto him, Get thee hence, Satan: for it is written, Thou shalt worship the Lord thy God, and him only shalt thou serve" (Matt. 10:8–10 KJV, emphasis mine).

Do you see how the number *forty* was used to point us to something that Jesus fulfilled? It is a pattern. Nothing in the Bible is written by accident. When a number in Scripture catches your attention, question it. Why did God put that number in this Scripture? Why is it important to know how many there are of such and such? If you don't ask questions, how will you ever find answers?

Finally, there is type and shadow. Type and shadow is a prophetic picture that comes from an actual event. Do you remember the story of Abraham when he offered Isaac up to be sacrificed? That was an actual event, but it was also prophetic of Jesus. How? Abraham represented Father God offering his only son on a sacrificial altar. Isaac (the promised seed), representing Jesus, carried the wood (the cross) up the hill. There was a substitution made on the altar. The substitution was Jesus dying in our place. There was also Abraham's expectation of Isaac's resurrection. In the same manner, Father God had faith in Jesus's resurrection.

"By faith Abraham, when he was tried, offered up Isaac: and he that had received the promises offered up his only begotten *son*, Of whom it was said, That in Isaac shall thy seed be called: *Accounting that God was able to raise him up, even from the dead; from whence also he received him in a figure*" (Heb. 11:17–19 KJV, emphasis mine).

Within this actual event is hidden the story of the Gospel. This is the how the Apostle Paul received the revelation of Scripture.

"Nevertheless death reigned from Adam to Moses, even over them that had not sinned after the similitude of Adam's transgression, *who is the figure (type or shadow) of him (Jesus) that was to come*" (Romans 5:14 KJV, emphasis mine).

Jesus is called "the last Adam" by the Apostle Paul (see 1 Corinth. 15:45 KJV).

"Not as though the word of God hath taken none effect. For they *are* not all Israel, which are of Israel: Neither, because they are the seed of Abraham, *are they* all children: but, In Isaac shall thy seed be called. That is, They which are the children of the flesh, these *are* not the children of God: but the children of the promise are counted for the seed. For this *is* the word of promise, At this time will I come, and Sara shall have a son. And not only *this*; but when Rebecca also had conceived by one, *even* by our father Isaac; (For *the children* being not yet born, neither having done any good or evil, that the purpose of God according to election might stand, not of works, but of him that calleth;) It was said unto her, The elder shall serve the younger. *As it is written, Jacob have I loved, but Esau have I hated*" (Romans 9:9–13 KJV, emphasis mine).

Notice how Paul based his doctrine on a type and shadow of Jacob and Esau. He used this to explain why the Gospel was going to the Gentiles. Jacob represents the Gentiles, and Esau represents the Jews. Esau sold his birthright to Jacob for food. Although it was only given to the firstborn, Esau did not value his birthright and gave it up for something temporary. The blessing was stolen from him through Jacob's deception.

The nation of Israel is God's firstborn son, birthed out of Egypt. The gospel went to Israel first by birthright. As a whole, the nation rejected it, and as a result, the blessing was taken from them and given to the Gentiles. Paul was given an abundance of revelation. Some people think that God "zapped" Paul with this abundance because he was called to be an apostle. We have to understand that Paul believed the religious traditions he learned from the Pharisees were correct and godly. He believed he was doing the will of God until Jesus knocked him off his horse on the road to Damascus. Paul's whole theological philosophy came crashing down. Can you imagine all the questions Paul had after that happened? He must have thought, Jesus is the Messiah and I am fighting against him—how wrong I have been for so long. Don't you think Paul began to search the Scriptures in order to understand how Jesus could be the Messiah? Of course he did. God gave the Apostle Paul *revelation from the Scripture*. When God gave Paul those revelations, do you think that Paul confirmed them in the Scriptures? Absolutely; there was no other way to know whether the revelations were true. Think about it. If Paul was teaching and preaching ideas not found in Scripture, no one would have believed him. Our only foundation for truth is Scripture. I can't stress that enough. I believe in dreams, visions, and visitations from the Lord, but they absolutely must line up with God's holy word. It is our standard. Today, we must confirm our doctrines by Scripture and Scripture alone. When we read the New Testament and the concepts therein, we should ask the question, where in the Old Testament did this come from? Why? In order to gain additional information on the concept or doctrine. And, you will also see the perspective of the writer of the Scripture, which will give you a more accurate interpretation. Later, we will use this to gain more understanding of the end times.

With these four rules or methods of interpretation, you can test a belief, and if it passes the test, it is absolute truth. Context will point you toward a belief. Confirmation by another clear Scripture will make it solid. Pattern and type and shadow will provide God's intent, additional information, and understanding of the established belief.

In the next chapter, we are going to take a look at the most popular end time teaching and try to understand it. You cannot evaluate something you do not fully understand. In this case, we will be examining the sensationalized pre-tribulation rapture theory.

Chapter 2

2

ROOT OF MODERN DAY PROPHECY

IN ORDER TO APPLY THE interpretation rules to the current and most popular prophecy teaching, we must understand the roots of the teaching. No, I am not going to chase rabbits about where this teaching originated or who believed it first. That is pointless and fruitless. What I am going to discuss is the *root*, or the *anchor*, of the current teaching. If the root is good, then the whole teaching will stand, but if not, it will tumble like a house of cards.

According to the current teaching, the rapture or "catching away" of the church occurs, and then the Antichrist comes to power and makes a covenant with Israel for seven years. Three and a half years into this covenant, the Antichrist breaks the covenant, stands in the rebuilt temple, and declares himself to be God. After that, God unleashes his wrath upon the earth for the last three and a half years of the seven-year tribulation. At the end of the seven-year tribulation, Jesus returns with his bride, destroying the armies that surrounded Israel during the battle of Armageddon. The Antichrist and the false prophet are then cast into the lake of fire. Immediately afterward, there is a thousand-year period during which Christ reigns on Earth and after which God creates a new heaven and new earth.

Wow, that is a mouthful! What is the root of this teaching? It is Daniel 9:24–27, the prophecy of the seventy weeks. The whole teaching cannot stand without this prophecy. If the modern day interpretation of Daniel 9:24-27 is correct, then the rest of the teaching has credence. If the interpretation is wrong, everything else in the teaching is false because it is all based on this Scripture. I want to explain how this prophecy is interpreted today, so we can clearly see where most prophecy teachers are coming from. Afterward, we will apply the rules of interpretation to it and see if it holds up.

"Seventy weeks are determined upon thy people and upon thy holy city, to finish the transgression, and to make an end of sins, and to make reconciliation for iniquity, and to bring in everlasting righteousness, and to seal up the vision and prophecy, and to anoint the most Holy. Know therefore and understand, *that* from the going forth of the commandment to restore and to build Jerusalem unto the Messiah the Prince *shall be* seven weeks, and threescore and two weeks: the street shall be built again, and the wall, even in troublous times. And after threescore and two weeks shall Messiah be cut off, but not for himself: and the people of the prince that shall come shall destroy the city and the sanctuary; and the end thereof *shall be* with a flood, and unto the end of the war desolations are determined. And he shall confirm the covenant with many for one week: and in the midst of the week he shall cause the sacrifice and the oblation to cease, and for the overspreading of abominations he shall make *it* desolate, even until the consummation, and that determined shall be poured upon the desolate"(Dan. 9:24–27 KJV).

"Seventy weeks are determined upon thy people and upon thy holy city..." Seventy weeks is being interpreted as seventy weeks of years (70 X 7) or 490 years. This 490-year period is for the people of Israel and the city of Jerusalem. At the end of the 490-year period, God will bring to pass the following:

+ Finish the transgression,
+ Make an end of sins,
+ Make reconciliation for iniquity,
+ Bring in everlasting righteousness,

+ Seal up the vision and prophecy,
+ Anoint the most holy.

According to current teaching, none of these have yet been accomplished. The reasoning is that this prophecy cannot have been completely fulfilled because sin, murder, thieves, and adulterers and so on are still present on the Earth. Additionally, the 490-year period gives the time when the Messiah would be cut off or crucified (483 years into the 490-year period). That part has been fulfilled. Jesus was crucified and is risen from the dead.

Because 483 years of this prophecy are believed to be complete and sin is still present on Earth, it is concluded that there must be a gap between the fulfillment of the 483 years and the last seven years. In other words, God's prophetic time clock stopped at the completion of the 483 years and will start again at a later date of God's choosing. The remaining seven years are known as the seven years of tribulation. Why tribulation? Verse 26 says that the people of the prince (taught as the Antichrist) would come and destroy the city (Jerusalem) and the sanctuary (the temple), and the desolations are determined. Verse 27 says He (the Antichrist) shall confirm the covenant with many for one week (seven years), and in the midst of the week (three and a half years), he (the Antichrist) will cause the sacrifice and oblation to cease and that which is determined shall be poured out on the desolate. In verse 27, there are sacrifices just as the Old Testament law demands. The conclusion made from this is that since the temple has been destroyed, another temple must be built in order for the Antichrist to cause the sacrifices to cease once again in the midst of the seven years of tribulation.

That is the basic interpretation of most popular prophecy teachers today. I'm sure they could add much more detail than I, but that is the gist of their interpretation. Is this teaching correct, or can you find holes in the interpretation? The answer may surprise you.

In my quest for the truth, I can't tell you how many times I questioned people about their end time belief system and they grew upset with me. Folks get touchy when it comes to certain beliefs, especially if they are unable to explain why they hold those beliefs in the first place. If you don't know why you believe what you believe, how do *you* know it's true? People are deceived by false doctrines all the time because they never question their own belief systems. Just because a pastor or trusted friend preaches and teaches a certain doctrine does not make it true. It is our responsibility *to rightly divide the word of truth* for ourselves to become the grounded, mature Christians God expects us to be. If you have been a Christian for a long time, I challenge you to go back to the Bible and act as though you don't know anything, asking God to show you the truth. He will confirm the truth and expose the lies. You will be surprised at what God will do.

Chapter 3

3

INTERPRETATION OR SPECULATION?

L ET'S BEGIN WITH THE METHOD used to interpret modern day teaching. The first method used to interpret Scripture is what can be seen in real life, sin. It is assumed, since we can still *see* sin on the Earth, the six things in Daniel 9:24 couldn't have come to pass:

+ Finish the transgression,
+ Make an end of sins,
+ Make reconciliation for iniquity,
+ Bring in everlasting righteousness,
+ Seal up the vision and prophecy,
+ Anoint the most holy.

The problem with this is we cannot judge the Scripture by the world. We must judge Scripture with Scripture. We must not *assume* something is true—it must be confirmed by Scripture. Many people *assume* that God does not heal today because *they* don't see any miracles. Scripture does not support this assumption. Our experiences do not prove anything about the Bible. For any teaching to progress, teachers should confirm and prove Scripture through Scripture.

Secondly, the "gap" in the fulfillment of this prophecy is the result of the previous assumption. Consequently, it is taught that part of the timed prophecy (490 years) has partially been fulfilled. If this is true, then there must be a precedent in Scripture. Did you know that the idea of precedent that is used in our court system today came from the Bible? A judge will decide a case based on a similar case that took place in the past. He has a precedent to go by. If there is a "gap" in the fulfillment of this prophecy, there should be another prophecy in which the same thing happens. To my knowledge, no other prophecy of this nature exists. Remember that these things must be confirmed, or they are not sound.

What about the covenant the Antichrist makes with Israel? It is shaky at best. The Scripture does not say that the Antichrist confirms a covenant with Israel. It says, "He shall confirm the covenant with many for one week." If "he" is the Antichrist, there must be more Scriptures that discuss this all-important event.

"And he *shall confirm the covenant with many* for one week: and in the midst of the week he shall cause the sacrifice and the oblation to cease, and for the overspreading of abominations he shall make *it* desolate, even until the consummation, and that determined shall be poured upon the desolate" (Dan. 9:26–27 KJV, emphasis mine).

"Many" is a far cry from stating Israel will be in covenant with the Antichrist. If these things are so, the Bible would absolutely confirm it! None of these beliefs have a second clear Scripture to confirm and establish them as true. Notice I said "clear" Scripture. It can't be vague or imprecise. There are Scriptures given by prophecy teachers to confirm these ideas, but you have to read a certain meaning into them rather than allowing the Scriptures to speak for themselves. Because of this, the rule of confirmation is violated. Did you notice how it is assumed that the "he" in verse 27 is the Antichrist without any real proof? If you can't absolutely prove that "he" is the Antichrist, do you have any business preaching that this as truth? We can't just say I think that's it and run with it. The principle of context is violated because of this lack of due diligence. In all the teachings I have heard, studied, and read, I have never seen a type or shadow revealing this scenario. In an event as big as the end of the world, you would think that God would have this spelled out in type and shadow prophecy. He does, but if you're always reading your own beliefs into the Scriptures, how can

God show you something different? There is a type and shadow of the end, but we will get into that later. It will show the truth very, very clearly. The pre-tribulational rapture theory does not have a type or shadow to confirm it, so that rule is also violated.

Finally, there is an attempt to use the numbers in the prophecy to explain the modern point of view, but the pattern is used incorrectly. The "gap theory," as I mentioned earlier, has no precedent in Scripture to back it up. Therefore, the rule of pattern concerning numbers is misused and violated. If you believe in the pre-tribulational rapture theory and think my assessment is incorrect, I challenge you to use these rules to establish your view. If you do apply these rules, you will discover the same things I discovered in the next chapter.

Chapter 4

4

SEVENTY WEEKS OF DANIEL: THE UNDENIABLE TRUTH

INTERPRETATION IS LIKE A JIGSAW puzzle. You should match up the ones that look alike, and then try to fit the pieces together without forcing them. Before you know it, you can see the parts of the picture for what they really are. Scripture can be viewed in much the same way. There is a piece here and a piece there, and suddenly, there is a vital doctrine founded and established before your very eyes. Like a jigsaw puzzle, we cannot force a doctrine to fit because this will distort the overall picture. If you try to force a false doctrine in with correct doctrines, you will receive an unclear and confusing overall view of the Bible and God. With that said, let's take a piece at a time and apply the rules to the text. Let's use context first.

You might want to get your Bible and refer back to Daniel 9:24–27 as I make observations about the prophecy. In order to begin on the right foot, I will start with the clearest points of the prophecy first. It is obvious that the Messiah (Jesus) is mentioned in the seventy weeks. That gives us a general time frame from which to work. The crucifixion of Christ is a centerpiece. For a starting point, I see the purpose of the prophecy is centered on Jesus and his sacrifice. Isn't the whole Bible centered on Jesus anyway? So, it's a good place to start. At the time this prophecy was given to Daniel, Israel had been conquered by the Babylonians because of their disobedience. Jerusalem and the temple had been destroyed and Daniel knew, through the writings of Jeremiah, that the desolations of Jerusalem and Israel were going to last for seventy years (see Daniel 9:1–19). Daniel inquired of the Lord what would happen to Israel and the city of Jerusalem. In the Lord's response, Gabriel said that Jerusalem, the street, and the wall would be built again in troublesome times (verse 25). In the next verse, the destruction of Jerusalem and the sanctuary is predicted. We can draw these two easy conclusions:

1. The prophecy is centered on Jesus and his crucifixion.
2. It predicts a second future destruction of Jerusalem and the temple (Judgment).

That's pretty basic and simple. I think sometimes people try to make interpretations too complex and make it hard for themselves. Just keep it simple.

The prophecy is based in the time period of Jesus because it predicts the time of his coming and crucifixion; therefore, it is safe to say that there *should* be a destruction of Jerusalem and the temple close to the time of Jesus. We know through history that Jerusalem and the temple were destroyed approximately forty years after the resurrection of Jesus. We have quickly seen the possible fulfillment date of this prophecy. It didn't require a theologian to help you see this, either. We used the basic rule of context to gather these easy conclusions. I see a clue to give us some insight and direction. History shows that there were approximately forty years between the resurrection and the destruction of Jerusalem and the temple. Remember that God uses numbers in pattern to give us additional information. Don't forget about those forty years—we will come back to that.

Previously, I stated that there is no precedent to assume that there is a "gap" in fulfillment during which the prophetic clock stops counting and starts again later. I personally have no knowledge of a precedent, but I could be wrong. It would be an assumption for me to just accept my position and move on. The burden of proof is on me.

To find this proof, I will look for a pattern in Scripture to confirm my theory. Remember that a pattern usually deals with numbers to point us toward a particular belief. The number we are interested in is 70 weeks, particularly, 70 weeks of years or 490 years. In Hebrew, this literally means seventy sevens or 70 x 7 equaling 490. One such pattern is found in the Exodus. If you begin counting from the first Passover to the day the twelve spies came back from observing the Promised Land, it is 490 days. Do your own independent research and confirm this for yourself. It's worth the time. Now that we have found the pattern number; let's see what we can learn from it. Since we have already established that the prophecy of the seventy weeks is centered on Jesus, we have to find Jesus somewhere in the pattern from Exodus to the spying out of the land. Remember type and shadow? Moses was a type and shadow of Jesus.

"The LORD thy God will raise up unto thee a Prophet from the midst of thee, of thy brethren, like unto me; unto him ye shall hearken; According to all that thou desiredst of the LORD thy God in Horeb in the day of the assembly, saying, Let me not hear again the voice of the LORD my God, neither let me see this great fire any more, that I die not. And the LORD said unto me, They have well spoken that which they have spoken. I will raise them up a Prophet from among their brethren, like unto thee, and will put my words in his mouth; and he shall speak unto them all that I shall command him"(Deut. 18:15–18 KJV, emphasis mine).

This Scripture is a direct prophecy of Jesus. Notice it said that the Prophet raised up by God would be like Moses. How is Jesus like Moses?

1. Moses spoke to God face to face. Jesus spoke to God face to face (he had no sin).
2. Moses delivered the Children of Israel out of Egypt, which was a type of sin. Jesus delivered us out of our sin.
3. Moses was the mediator between the children of Israel and God. Jesus is our mediator.
4. Moses's ministry was characterized by many miracles and provisions of God. Jesus's ministry was full of the same.
5. Moses listened to God and built the first tabernacle. Jesus said, tear down this temple and I will raise it up in three days, meaning the tabernacle of his body.

6. Israel rejected God, Moses, and the Word of the Lord when the spies returned from the promise land. The religious leaders rejected Jesus and had him crucified.

Can you see the similarities? Now, let's confirm this with another Scripture.

"And *he shall send Jesus Christ,* which before was preached unto you: Whom the heaven must receive until the times of restitution of all things, which God hath spoken by the mouth of all his holy prophets since the world began. *For Moses truly said unto the fathers, A prophet shall the Lord your God raise up unto you* of your brethren, like unto me; him shall ye hear in all things whatsoever he shall say unto you"(Acts 3:19–22 KJV, emphasis mine).

Peter referenced this verse and directly said that Jesus is the prophet whom the Lord would raise up. We have a match. Let's continue.

We begin counting the 490-day period with Moses on the first Passover, when the Israelites were delivered from bondage. If we follow the pattern, the first day of the 490-year period must start off with deliverance from bondage.

"*Know therefore and understand, that from the going forth of the commandment to restore and to build Jerusalem unto the Messiah* the Prince *shall be* seven weeks, and threescore and two weeks: the street shall be built again, and the wall, even in troublous times"(Dan. 9:24–25 KJV, emphasis mine).

Note that the beginning of the 490-year period in Daniel starts at the release of some Israelites who were to go back to Jerusalem and restore and build Jerusalem. This is deliverance back to Israel. The beginnings of both match perfectly. The prophecy in Daniel does not mention anything happening in the middle of the 490-year period, so let's go to the end to see if they match.

At the end of the 490-day period with Moses, the twelve spies returned from the Promised Land and all but two argued that they were not able to take the land. Because of their unbelief, a declaration of Judgment was passed on that generation. Through Moses, God declared that this particular generation would not enter the Promised Land and would die in the wilderness. Over the next 40 years, it came to pass that everyone 20 years and older died in the wilderness. Here, we see the number 40 again. At the end of the 490-day period, the judgment was set and then 40 years passed before it was fully realized. Let's look at this pattern in Jesus's day. We know that the 490-year period had to end close to the time of Jesus's death because it predicts his crucifixion. If that is true, was a judgment set at the time of Jesus's death? Yes! The crucifixion of Jesus set the course for Israel. They rejected their Messiah, and destruction would follow because of that.

"Then certain of the scribes and of the Pharisees answered, saying, Master, we would see a sign from thee. But he answered and said unto them, *An evil and adulterous generation seeketh* after a sign; and there shall no sign be given to it, but the sign of the prophet Jonas: For as Jonas was three days and three nights in the whale's belly; so shall the Son of man be three days and three nights in the heart of the earth. The men of Nineveh shall *rise in judgment with this generation, and shall condemn it*: because they repented at the preaching of Jonas; and, behold, a greater than Jonas *is* here. The queen of the south shall *rise up in the judgment with this generation, and shall condemn it*: For she came from the uttermost parts of the earth to hear the Wisdom of Solomon; and, behold, a greater than Solomon *is* here. When the unclean spirit is gone out of a man, he walketh through dry places, seeking rest, and findeth none. Then he saith, I will return into my house from whence I came out; and when he is come, he findeth *it* empty, swept, and garnished. Then goeth he, and taketh with himself seven other spirits more wicked than himself, and they enter in and dwell there: and the last *state* of that man is worse than the first. *Even so shall it be also unto this wicked generation*" (Matt. 12:38–45 KJV, emphasis mine).

"Every valley shall be filled, and every mountain and hill shall be brought low; and the crooked shall be made straight, and the rough ways *shall be* made smooth; And all flesh shall see the salvation of God. Then said he to the multitude that came forth to be baptized of him, *O generation of vipers, who hath warned you to flee from the wrath to come?* Bring forth therefore fruits worthy of repentance, and begin not to say within yourselves, We have

Abraham to *our* father: for I say unto you, That God is able of these stones to raise up children unto Abraham. *And now also the axe is laid unto the root of the trees: every tree therefore which bringeth not forth good fruit is hewn down, and cast into the fire*" (Luke 3:5–9 KJV, emphasis mine).

"And when the people were gathered thick together, he began to say, *This is an evil generation:* they seek a sign; and there shall no sign be given it, but the sign of Jonas the prophet. For as Jonas was a sign unto the Ninevites, *so shall also the Son of man be to this generation.* The queen of the south shall *rise up in the judgment with the men of this generation, and condemn them:* for she came from the utmost parts of the earth to hear the wisdom of Solomon; and, behold, a greater than Solomon *is* here. The men of *Nineve shall rise up in the judgment with this generation, and shall condemn it:* for they repented at the preaching of Jonas; and, behold, a greater than Jonas *is* here" (Luke 11:29–32 KJV, emphasis mine).

"There were present at that season some that told him of the Galilaeans, whose blood Pilate had mingled with their sacrifices. And Jesus answering said unto them, Suppose ye that these Galilaeans were sinners above all the Galilaeans, because they suffered such things? *I tell you, Nay: but, except ye repent, ye shall all likewise perish. Or those eighteen, upon whom the tower in Siloam fell, and slew them, think ye that they were sinners above all men that dwelt in Jerusalem?* I tell you, Nay: but, except ye repent, ye shall all likewise perish.

He spake also this parable; A certain *man* had a fig tree planted in his vineyard; and he came and sought fruit thereon, and found none. Then said he unto the dresser of his vineyard, Behold, these three years I come seeking fruit on this fig tree, and find none: cut it down; why cumbereth it the ground? And he answering said unto him, Lord, let it alone this year also, till I shall dig about it, and dung *it: And if it bear fruit, well: and if not, then after that thou shalt cut it down*" (Luke 13:1–9 KJV, emphasis mine).

The fig tree in this parable is Israel. They did not bear fruit and were cut down. This sheds light on why Jesus said:

"Now learn a parable of the fig tree; When his branch is yet tender, and putteth forth leaves, ye know that summer *is* nigh: So likewise ye, when ye shall see all these things, know that it is near, *even* at the doors. Verily I say unto you, *This generation shall not pass, till all these things be fulfilled"* (Matt. 24:32–34 KJV, emphasis mine).

You can clearly see that Jesus gets this from the pattern. He knew that the generation to whom he was speaking would die in the wilderness, spiritually speaking. He also knew that Jerusalem and the temple would be destroyed during that generation (see Matt 24:2). Jesus plainly told the Pharisees this.

"Hear another parable: There was a certain householder, which planted a vineyard, and hedged it round about, and digged a winepress in it, and built a tower, and let it out to husbandmen, and went into a far country: And when the time of the fruit drew near, he sent his servants to the husbandmen, that they might receive the fruits of it. And the husbandmen took his servants, and beat one, and killed another, and stoned another. Again, he sent other servants more than the first: and they did unto them likewise. But last of all he sent unto them his son, saying, They will reverence my son. But when the husbandmen saw the son, they said among themselves, This is the heir; come, let us kill him, and let us seize on his inheritance. And they caught him, and cast *him* out of the vineyard, and slew *him*. When the lord therefore of the vineyard cometh, what will he do unto those husbandmen? *They say unto him, He will miserably destroy those wicked men, and will let out his vineyard unto other husbandmen, which shall render him the fruits in their seasons. Jesus saith unto them, Did ye never read in the Scriptures, The stone which the builders rejected, the same is become the head of the corner: this is the Lord's doing, and it is marvellous in our eyes? Therefore say I unto you, The kingdom of God shall be taken from you, and given to a nation bringing forth the fruits thereof. And whosoever shall fall on this stone shall be broken: but on whomsoever it shall fall, it will grind him to powder.* And when the chief priests and Pharisees had heard his parables, they perceived that he spake of them" (Matt. 21:33–45 KJV, emphasis mine).

The kingdom of God was taken from Israel during 70 A.D. at the destruction of the temple and given to a holy nation that would bring forth the fruits thereof. That nation is called the Church. God poured out his wrath on Israel and miserably destroyed them just as the Pharisees suggested.

Now, where did Jesus get that parable? Did he just make it up? Remember when I said that you can gain additional information if you ask where something comes from in the Old Testament? This is such a case. In fact, by looking back to the Old Testament, you get to see what Jesus was thinking about when he spoke that parable!

"Now will I sing to my wellbeloved a song of my beloved touching his *vineyard. My wellbeloved hath a vineyard in a very fruitful hill: And he fenced it, and gathered out the stones thereof, and planted it with the choicest vine, and built a tower in the midst of it, and also made a winepress therein*: and he looked that it should bring forth grapes, and it brought forth wild grapes" (Isaiah 5:1–2 KJV, emphasis mine).

Does that sound familiar? Jesus had Isaiah 5 in mind when he told that parable. In Isaiah, you can read about the destruction and fall of Jerusalem. I hope you are at least half as excited about this as I am!

"And now, O inhabitants of Jerusalem, and men of Judah, judge, I pray you, betwixt me and my vineyard. What could have been done more to my vineyard, that I have not done in it? wherefore, when I looked that it should bring forth grapes, brought it forth wild grapes? And now go to; I will tell you what I will do to my vineyard: I will take away the hedge thereof, and it shall be eaten up; *and* break down the wall thereof, and it shall be trodden down: And I will lay it waste: it shall not be pruned, nor digged; but there shall come up briers and thorns: I will also command the clouds that they rain no rain upon it. *For the vineyard of the LORD of hosts is the house of Israel*, and the men of Judah his pleasant plant: and he looked for judgment, but behold oppression; for righteousness, but behold a cry.

Woe unto them that join house to house, *that* lay field to field, till *there be* no place, that they may be placed alone in the midst of the earth! In mine ears *said* the LORD of hosts, Of a truth many houses shall be desolate, *even* great and fair, without inhabitant. Yea, ten acres of vineyard shall yield one bath, and the seed of an homer shall yield an ephah. Woe unto them that rise up early in the morning, *that* they may follow strong drink; that continue until night, *till* wine inflame them! And the harp, and the viol, the tabret, and pipe, and wine, are in their feasts: but they regard not the work of the LORD, neither consider the operation of his hands. Therefore my people are gone into captivity, because *they have* no knowledge: and their honourable men *are* famished, and their multitude dried up with thirst. Therefore hell hath enlarged herself, and opened her mouth without measure: and their glory, and their multitude, and their pomp, and he that rejoiceth, shall descend into it. And the mean man shall be brought down, and the mighty man shall be humbled, and the eyes of the lofty shall be humbled: But the LORD of hosts shall be exalted in judgment, and God that is holy shall be sanctified in righteousness. Then shall the lambs feed after their manner, and the waste places of the fat ones shall strangers eat.

Woe unto them that draw iniquity with cords of vanity, and sin as it were with a cart rope: That say, Let him make speed, *and* hasten his work, that we may see *it*: and let the counsel of the Holy One of Israel draw nigh and come, that we may know *it*! Woe unto them that call evil good, and good evil; that put darkness for light, and light for darkness; that put bitter for sweet, and sweet for bitter! Woe unto *them that are* wise in their own eyes, and prudent in their own sight! Woe unto *them that are* mighty to drink wine, and men of strength to mingle strong drink: Which justify the wicked for reward, and take away the righteousness of the righteous from him! Therefore as the fire devoureth the stubble, and the flame consumeth the chaff, *so* their root shall be as rottenness, and their blossom shall go up as dust: because they have cast away the law of the LORD of hosts, and despised the word of the Holy One of Israel. Therefore is the anger of the LORD kindled against his people, and he hath stretched forth his hand against them, and hath smitten them: and the hills did tremble, and their carcases *were* torn in the midst of the streets. For all this his anger is not turned away, but his hand *is* stretched out still. And he will lift up an ensign to the nations from far, and will hiss unto them from the end of the earth: and, behold, they shall come with speed swiftly: None shall be weary nor stumble among them; none shall slumber nor sleep; neither shall the girdle of their loins be loosed, nor the latchet of their shoes be broken: Whose arrows *are* sharp, and all their bows bent, their horses' hoofs shall be counted like flint, and their wheels like a whirlwind: Their roaring *shall be* like a lion, they shall roar like young lions: yea, they shall roar, and lay hold of the prey, and shall carry *it* away safe, and none shall deliver *it*. And in that day they shall roar against them like the roaring of the sea: and if *one* look unto the land, behold darkness *and* sorrow, and the light is darkened in the heavens thereof" (Isaiah 5:3–30 KJV, emphasis mine).

Now think about this: didn't Daniel 9:24–27 also mention the destruction of Jerusalem and the sanctuary, and that the determined would be poured out upon the desolate? It sure did. The whole pattern fits.

"And after threescore and two weeks shall Messiah be cut off, but not for himself: *and the people of the prince that shall come shall destroy the city and the sanctuary; and the end thereof shall be with a flood, and unto the end of the war desolations are determined.* And he shall confirm the covenant with many for one week: *and in the midst of the week he shall cause the sacrifice and the oblation to cease, and for the overspreading of abominations he shall make it desolate, even until the consummation, and that determined shall be poured upon the desolate*" (Dan. 9:25–27 KJV, emphasis mine).

The sacrifice and oblation ended with the destruction of Jerusalem and the temple. The desolate described here were the unbelievers among the Jews who rejected Jesus and were still looking for the Messiah to come. This means that "the people of the prince" who were supposed to destroy Jerusalem and the temple had to be the Romans, not the Antichrist.

This type and shadow and pattern show the true interpretation of Daniel's seventy weeks without a "gap" in fulfillment. To recap, a 490-year countdown started at the command to restore and rebuild Jerusalem. At the end of this time period, the Messiah was supposed to appear, and Jesus did appear. When Jesus was rejected and crucified, a judgment was placed on that generation, to "die in the spiritual wilderness." At the end of this generation, Jerusalem and the temple were destroyed—40 years later. Please, go back and study these things before we continue on to the next chapter. Be blessed.

Chapter 5

WHAT JESUS TAUGHT ABOUT
THE SEVENTY WEEKS OF DANIEL

CHANCES ARE YOU ARE PROBABLY in awe of how simple interpreting
Scripture in this manner really is. It does take time to search out, but
when you finish, it will be accurate. Rely on the Holy Spirit to lead you and
enlighten your mind with the thoughts and ideas necessary to rightly divide
the word of Truth.

If you have fully followed this line of logic, you can see how each piece
fits together with the next. When the right pieces are put in the right places,
a picture can be seen. Isn't it amazing how exact the pattern is? Now, do
you see any pattern like this in any other end time teaching? I think not.
I am not here to condemn prophecy teachers, but to show how to prove
truth, because that is what is needed. Confirmation through Old Testament
types and shadows is how Jesus, Paul, and many other writers in the New
Testament showed the truth of Jesus as Messiah and many other important
doctrines. My prayer is that this book will be used to open eyes to see that
we can absolutely verify and present Gospel Truth, instead of speculation.
Let me step down from my soapbox and we will continue.

What I am about to share with you is something that puzzled me for
a long time. I knew there had to be more to this issue than I understood at
the time. You have probably heard as many countless sermons on this text
as I have. Although in most cases, the truth was presented, during these

sermons, I kept having a strong feeling that a deeper revelation was waiting to be discovered. Here is the text.

"Moreover if thy brother shall trespass against thee, go and tell him his fault between thee and him alone: if he shall hear thee, thou hast gained thy brother. But if he will not hear *thee, then* take with thee one or two more, that in the mouth of two or three witnesses every word may be established. And if he shall neglect to hear them, tell *it* unto the church: but if he neglect to hear the church, let him be unto thee as an heathen man and a publican. Verily I say unto you, Whatsoever ye shall bind on earth shall be bound in heaven: and whatsoever ye shall loose on earth shall be loosed in heaven. Again I say unto you, That if two of you shall agree on earth as touching any thing that they shall ask, it shall be done for them of my Father which is in heaven. For where two or three are gathered together in my name, there am I in the midst of them.

Then came Peter to him, and said, Lord, how oft shall my brother sin against me, and I forgive him? till seven times? Jesus saith unto him, I say not unto thee, Until seven times: but, Until seventy times seven" (Matt. 18:15–22 KJV).

Jesus is teaching on forgiveness and how to handle someone who has sinned against you. Peter, with his curious nature, asks how many times he should forgive, seven times? Jesus's response has always seemed strange to me. Jesus said, forgive seventy times seven. Why would Jesus say to forgive 490 times? I've heard preachers say that Jesus chose that number because it shows an infinite amount of forgiveness. I think we should dig a little deeper to find the answer.

Up until now, we have used the four rules of interpretation to gain true knowledge of Scripture. Which rule do you think we should apply here? If you said pattern, you are correct.

One question we have to answer is why Jesus said to forgive 490 times. If this is a pattern, then the same number can be found in other places in Scripture. Because of our previous study, we know it is found in the seventy weeks of Daniel. Another question we have to answer is why Jesus linked forgiveness to 490.

The rule of pattern sends us back to Daniel for the answer, but we must use the rule of context to understand the links between forgiveness, the number 490, and the seventy weeks of Daniel.

"In the first year of Darius the son of Ahasuerus, of the seed of the Medes, which was made king over the realm of the Chaldeans; In the first year of his reign I Daniel understood by books the number of the years, whereof the word of the LORD came to Jeremiah the prophet, that he would accomplish seventy years in the desolations of Jerusalem. And I set my face unto the Lord God, to seek by prayer and supplications, with fasting, and sackcloth, and ashes" (Dan. 9:1–3 KJV).

We see Daniel seeking God by prayer and supplication, with fasting, sackcloth, and ashes. Daniel is praying because Jerusalem had been destroyed and the people had been carried off into Babylon. It had been nearly 70 years since this began. From the writings of Jeremiah, Daniel knows that God would restore Israel after 70 years. Daniel is praying to find out when this will begin, and in the next few verses, he repents on behalf of Israel.

"And I prayed unto the LORD my God, and made my confession, and said, O Lord, the great and dreadful God, keeping the covenant and mercy to them that love him, and to them that keep his commandments; We have sinned, and have committed iniquity, and have done wickedly, and have rebelled, even by departing from thy precepts and from thy judgments: Neither have we hearkened unto thy servants the prophets, which spake in thy name to our kings, our princes, and our fathers, and to all the people of the land. O Lord, righteousness *belongeth* unto thee, but unto us confusion of faces, as at this day; to the men of Judah, and to the inhabitants of Jerusalem, and unto all Israel, *that are* near, and *that are* far off, through all the countries whither thou hast driven them, because of their trespass that they have trespassed against thee. O Lord, to us *belongeth* confusion of face, to our kings, to our princes, and to our fathers, because we have sinned against thee. To the Lord our God *belong* mercies and forgivenesses, though we have rebelled against him; Neither have we obeyed the voice of the LORD our God, to walk in his laws, which he set before us by his servants the prophets. Yea, all Israel have transgressed thy law, even by departing, that they might not obey thy voice; therefore the curse is poured upon us, and the oath that *is* written in the law of Moses the servant of God, because we have sinned against him. And he hath confirmed his words, which he spake against us, and against our judges that judged us, by bringing upon us a great evil: for under the whole heaven hath not been done as hath been done upon Jerusalem. As *it is* written in the law of Moses, all this evil is come upon us: yet made we not our prayer before the LORD our God, that we might turn from our iniquities, and understand thy truth. Therefore hath the LORD watched upon the evil, and brought it upon us: for the LORD our God *is* righteous in all his works which he doeth: for we obeyed not his voice. And now, O Lord our God, that hast brought thy people forth out of the land of Egypt with a mighty hand, and hast gotten thee renown, as at this day; we have sinned, we have done wickedly. O Lord, according to all thy righteousness, I beseech thee, let thine anger and thy fury be turned away from thy city Jerusalem, thy holy mountain: because for our sins, and for the iniquities of our fathers, Jerusalem and thy people *are become* a reproach to all *that are* about us. Now therefore, O our God, hear the prayer of thy servant, and his supplications, and cause thy face to shine upon thy sanctuary that is desolate, for the Lord's sake. O my God, incline thine ear, and hear; open thine eyes, and behold our desolations, and the city which is called by thy name: for we do not present our supplications before thee for our righteousnesses, but for thy great mercies. O Lord, hear; O Lord, forgive; O Lord, hearken and do; defer not, for thine own sake, O my God: for thy city and thy people are called by thy name" (Dan. 9:4–19 KJV).

Daniel asks God to forgive Israel, restore the people to Jerusalem, and rebuild the city and the sanctuary. I want you to notice how God responds to Daniel.

"And whiles I *was* speaking, and praying, and confessing my sin and the sin of my people Israel, and presenting my supplication before the LORD my God for the holy mountain of my God; Yea, whiles I *was* speaking in prayer, even the man Gabriel, whom I had seen in the vision at the beginning, being caused to fly swiftly, touched me about the time of the evening oblation. And he informed *me*, and talked with me, and said, O Daniel, I am now come forth to give thee skill and understanding. At the beginning of thy supplications the commandment came forth, and I am come to shew *thee*;

for thou *art* greatly beloved: therefore understand the matter, and consider the vision. Seventy weeks are determined upon thy people and upon thy holy city, to finish the transgression, and to make an end of sins, and to make reconciliation for iniquity, and to bring in everlasting righteousness, and to seal up the vision and prophecy, and to anoint the most Holy"(Dan. 9:20–24 KJV).

The Scripture points out that as Daniel was still praying, Gabriel appeared to him. Gabriel says, I am come to give you understanding, consider the vision. Gabriel then says, "Seventy weeks are determined upon thy people and upon thy holy city." God's response to Daniel's prayer was the vision of the seventy weeks.

Now, let us get this straight: Daniel is praying for forgiveness, and God's response was the vision of the seventy weeks. Did they receive forgiveness? Yes, because God promised to restore the people back to Israel and rebuild the city, the wall, and the sanctuary. We can see now why Jesus links forgiveness to the number 490. Let's move on to the other question, why did Jesus say to forgive 490 times?

Is this indicating to us that Father God forgave Israel 490 times, starting at the command to restore? Why wouldn't God just forgive them once and be done with it? The answer to that is found in Leviticus.

"And he shall make *an atonement* for the holy sanctuary, and he shall make an atonement for the tabernacle of the congregation, and for the altar, and he shall make an atonement for the priests, and for all the people of the congregation. And this shall be an everlasting statute unto you, to make an atonement for the children of *Israel for all their sins once a year.* And he did as the LORD commanded Moses" (Lev. 16:33–34 KJV, emphasis mine).

Did you understand that? God forgave them for all their sins once a year. If you begin at the command to rebuild and restore and count out 490 years, it will end about the time Jesus was crucified. How do I know God no longer offered forgiveness? It's not that God quit forgiving, but that forgiveness was offered in a different form. Here's what I mean. God provided forgiveness through the sacrifice of a spotless lamb that was offered once a year for the atonement of sin. Then Jesus was offered on the cross as THE spotless lamb of God. Forgiveness was no longer offered through the sacrifice of a lamb as it was in the Old Testament. The offering of Jesus changed the acceptable way to receive forgiveness from God. Israel as a nation rejected Jesus as their Messiah. Only a remnant received Jesus as Messiah. Because of this, Israel was made subject to judgment. How? Israel had no more covering for sin.

"But all these things will they do unto you for my name's sake, because they know not him that sent me. *If I had not come and spoken unto them, they had not had sin: but now they have no cloke for their sin.* He that hateth me hateth my Father also. *If I had not done among them the works which none other man did, they had not had sin:* but now have they both seen and hated both me and my Father. But *this cometh to pass,* that the word might be fulfilled that is written in their law, They hated me without a cause" (John 15:20–25 KJV, emphasis mine).

Jesus said, if I had not come and spoken to them, they would have no sin. Why? They would still have the sacrificial system in place. Jesus's teaching and the works he did were a testimony to the fact that he was the Messiah.

"Jesus answered them, I told you, and ye believed not: *the works* that I do in my Father's name, *they bear witness of me*" (John 10:25 KJV, emphasis mine).

Their sin remained because they rejected Jesus as Messiah. Israel as a nation lay in sin when they rejected Jesus, and therefore, God was obligated to judge that sin. That's why this was the end of the 490-year period when forgiveness was no longer extended to those who were still operating under Old Testament law. This rejection (the crucifixion of Jesus) marked the beginning of that generation "dying in the wilderness" and "not entering into the promised land," just like the pattern set with Moses and the children of Israel. Judgment was passed on Israel because they rejected their own forgiveness, culminating in the final destruction of the temple system. Isaiah prophesied about God's feelings toward the sacrifices after Jesus. In order to know that the next Scripture applies in Jesus's time period, let's look at how Jesus used Isaiah's writings in his time.

"Well hath *Esaias prophesied of you hypocrites,* as it is written, This people honoureth me with *their* lips, but their heart is far from me. Howbeit in vain do they worship me, teaching *for* doctrines the commandments of men" (Mark 7:6–7 KJV, emphasis mine).

Notice how Jesus used this quote from Isaiah to apply to the Pharisees in Jesus's day. It originally applied to Israel in Isaiah's time period, but there was a duel fulfillment—one fulfillment in both time periods. The Scripture you are about to read also has a duel fulfillment. The first fulfillment happened when the first sanctuary was destroyed with the fall of Israel to Babylon, and the second occurred in Jesus's day. I want you to see how these verses apply to Israel during the rejection of Jesus and the results of that act.

"The vision of Isaiah the son of Amoz, which he saw concerning *Judah and Jerusalem* in the days of Uzziah, Jotham, Ahaz, *and* Hezekiah, kings of Judah. Hear, O heavens, and give ear, O earth: for the LORD hath spoken, I have nourished and brought up children, *and they have rebelled against me.* The ox knoweth his owner, and the ass his master's crib: *but Israel doth not know, my people doth not consider*" (Isaiah 1:1–3 KJV, emphasis mine).

Rejection of God is declared here—Israel had forgotten God.

"Ah sinful nation, a people laden with iniquity, a seed of evildoers, children that are corrupters: they have forsaken the LORD, they have provoked the Holy One of Israel unto anger, they are gone away backward. Why should ye be stricken any more? ye will revolt more and more: the whole head is sick, and the whole heart faint. From the sole of the foot even unto the head *there is* no soundness in it; *but* wounds, and bruises, and putrefying sores: they have not been closed, neither bound up, neither mollified with ointment" (Isaiah 1:4–6 KJV).

God expresses his disgust with Israel.

"*Your country is desolate, your cities are burned with fire: your land, strangers devour it in your presence, and it is desolate,* as overthrown by strangers. And the daughter of Zion is left as a cottage in a vineyard, as a lodge in a garden of cucumbers, *as a besieged city*" (Isaiah 1:7–8 KJV, emphasis mine).

God mentions the destruction and desolation of Israel and how they are conquered by strangers.

"Except the LORD of *hosts had left unto us a very small remnant,* we should have been as Sodom, *and we should have been like unto Gomorrah*" (Isaiah 1:9 KJV, emphasis mine).

The remnant left were those who accepted the sacrifice of Jesus. Much more can be said about this, and we will return to it later.

"Hear the word of the LORD, ye rulers of Sodom; give ear unto the law of our God, ye people of Gomorrah" (Isaiah 1:10 KJV).

God calls them spiritual Sodom and Gomorrah, meaning they are deserving of judgment.

"To what purpose *is* the multitude of your sacrifices unto me? saith the LORD: I am full of the burnt offerings of rams, and the fat of fed beasts; and I delight not in the blood of bullocks, or of lambs, or of he goats. When ye come to appear before me, who hath required this at your hand, to tread my courts? *Bring no more vain oblations; incense is an abomination unto me; the new moons and sabbaths, the calling of assemblies, I cannot away with; it is iniquity, even the solemn meeting. Your new moons and your appointed feasts my soul hateth: they are a trouble unto me; I am weary to bear them.* And when ye spread forth your hands, I will hide mine eyes from you: yea, when ye make many prayers, *I will not hear: your hands are full of blood*" (Isaiah 1:10–15 KJV).

Did you notice the relationship between the Besieged city (Jerusalem) and the disgust that God had for the sacrifices and the laws they were following? That disgust was caused by their disobedience and rejection of God. Let's continue.

"*Wash you, make you clean; put away the evil of your doings from before mine eyes; cease to do evil;* Learn to do well; seek judgment, relieve the oppressed, judge the fatherless, plead for the widow. Come now, and let us reason together, saith the LORD: *though your sins be as scarlet, they shall be as white as snow; though they be red like crimson, they shall be as wool*" (Isaiah 1:16–18 KJV, emphasis mine).

"Wash you, make you clean...though your sins be as scarlet, they shall be as white as snow." That sounds like the cleansing of sin through the blood of Jesus, doesn't it?

"If ye be willing and obedient, ye shall eat the good of the land: *But if ye refuse and rebel, ye shall be devoured with the sword:* for the mouth of the LORD hath spoken *it*" (Isaiah 1:19–20 KJV, emphasis mine).

God is pleading with them to forget the sacrifices and learn the weightier things, the things Jesus did, such as learning to do well, seeking judgment, relieving the oppressed, judging the fatherless, and pleading for widows. God desires them to obey and to be cleansed of their sins.

This is a prophecy of how God despised animal sacrifices after Jesus was crucified, and how God would judge them if Israel did not repent. And, that is exactly what God did.

We have seen why Jesus used 490 as the number of times to forgive. We have also seen why Jesus linked 490 to forgiveness itself. Let's go back to Matthew 18 and see what else Jesus says after his conversation with Peter. If the scenario I have presented is true, then it should fall in line with the following parable.

"Therefore is the kingdom of heaven likened unto a certain king, *which would take account of his servants. And when he had begun to reckon,* one was brought unto him, which owed him ten thousand talents" (Matt. 18:22–24 KJV, emphasis mine).

In the time of Isaiah, Israel was in disobedience. They refused to listen to God and his prophets, who warned them of the judgment that would happen unless they repented. Israel turned to other gods and even killed some of God's prophets because of their message. The Babylonian empire was coming to conquer Israel. It was God's judgment on them for their disobedience. It was a time of reckoning for them. In essence, God was settling his account with Israel. In the following parable, Israel is the one that owed the great amount of ten thousand talents.

"But forasmuch as he had not to pay, his lord commanded him to be sold, and his wife, and children, and all that he had, and payment to be made" (Matt. 18:25 KJV).

Israel could not pay their debt of sin, so payment was made in the form of slavery in Babylon for seventy years. After seventy years, Daniel began to pray and repent for Israel, and God answered him. God forgave Israel and allowed them to go back to their homeland.

"The servant therefore fell down, and worshipped him, saying, Lord, have patience with me, and I will pay thee all. Then the lord of that servant was moved with compassion, and loosed him, and forgave him the debt" (Matt. 18:26–27 KJV).

Israel went back to their land and rebuilt the wall, Jerusalem, and the temple destroyed by the Babylonians. The destruction of Jerusalem and the sanctuary was part of the payment that the Lord required of them. However, after their return, Israel did not change their ways. They were still hardhearted, dull of hearing, and selfish. Their religious leaders looked down on the common people of Israel, and instead of loving their neighbors, they despised them. They refused to forgive their debt!

"But the same servant went out, and found one of his fellowservants, which owed him an hundred pence: and he laid hands on him, and took *him* by the throat, saying, Pay me that thou owest. And his fellowservant fell down at his feet, and besought him, saying, Have patience with me, and I will pay thee all. And he would not: but went and cast him into prison, till he should pay the debt" (Matt. 18:27–30 KJV).

God had forgiven the debt of Israel, but they did not change, and God responded by judging them once again. If the first judgment destroyed Jerusalem and the temple, the second judgment should be the same. Forty years after the resurrection of Jesus, Jerusalem and the temple were destroyed again. Jesus was warning that generation of this judgment.

"And his fellowservant fell down at his feet, and besought him, saying, Have patience with me, and I will pay thee all. And he would not: but went and cast him into prison, till he should pay the debt. So when his fellowservants saw what was done, they were very sorry, and came and told unto their lord all that was done. Then his lord, after that he had called him, said unto him, O thou wicked servant, I forgave thee all that debt, because thou desiredst me: Shouldest not thou also have had compassion on thy fellowservant, even as I had pity on thee? *And his lord was wroth, and delivered him to the tormentors, till he should pay all that was due unto him. So* likewise shall my heavenly Father do also unto you, if ye from your hearts forgive not every one his brother their trespasses" (Matt. 18:29–35 KJV, emphasis mine).

In both judgments, Israel was defeated in battle and scattered throughout the nations, and Jerusalem and the temple were destroyed. Let's confirm this by discovering the nature of the debt that Israel owed.

"Then spake Jesus to the multitude, and to his disciples, Saying, The scribes and the Pharisees sit in Moses' seat: All therefore whatsoever they bid you observe, *that* observe and do; but do not ye after their works: for they say, and do not. For they bind heavy burdens and grievous to be borne, and lay *them* on men's shoulders; but they *themselves* will not move them with one of their fingers. But all their works they do for to be seen of men: they make broad their phylacteries, and enlarge the borders of their garments, And love the uppermost rooms at feasts, and the chief seats in the synagogues, And greetings in the markets, and to be called of men, Rabbi, Rabbi. But be not ye called Rabbi: for one is your Master, *even* Christ; and all ye are brethren. And call no *man* your father upon the earth: for one is your Father, which is in heaven. Neither be ye called masters: for one is your Master, *even* Christ. But he that is greatest among you shall be your servant. And whosoever shall exalt himself shall be abased; and he that shall humble himself shall be exalted.

But woe unto you, scribes and Pharisees, hypocrites! for ye shut up the kingdom of heaven against men: for ye neither go in *yourselves*, neither suffer ye them that are entering to go in. Woe unto you, scribes and Pharisees, hypocrites! for ye devour widows' houses, and for a pretence make long prayer: therefore ye shall receive the greater damnation. Woe unto you, scribes and Pharisees, hypocrites! for ye compass sea and land to make one proselyte, and when he is made, ye make him twofold more the child of hell than yourselves. Woe unto you, *ye* blind guides, which say, Whosoever shall swear by the temple, it is nothing; but whosoever shall swear by the gold of the temple, he is a debtor! *Ye* fools and blind: for whether is greater, the gold, or the temple that sanctifieth the gold? And, Whosoever shall swear by the altar, it is nothing; but whosoever sweareth by the gift that is upon it, he is guilty. *Ye* fools and blind: for whether *is* greater, the gift, or the altar that sanctifieth the gift? Whoso therefore shall swear by the altar, sweareth by it, and by all things thereon. And whoso shall swear by the temple, sweareth by it, and by him that dwelleth therein. And he that shall swear by heaven, sweareth by the throne of God, and by him that sitteth thereon. Woe unto you, scribes and Pharisees, hypocrites! for ye pay tithe of mint and anise and cummin, and have omitted the weightier *matters* of the law, judgment, mercy, and faith: these ought ye to have done, and not to leave the other undone. *Ye* blind guides, which strain at a gnat, and swallow a camel. Woe unto you, scribes and Pharisees, hypocrites! for ye make clean the outside of the cup and of the platter, but within they are full of extortion and excess. *Thou* blind Pharisee, cleanse first that *which is* within the cup and platter, that the outside of them may be clean also. Woe unto you, scribes and Pharisees, hypocrites! for ye are like unto whited sepulchres, which indeed appear beautiful outward, but are within full of dead *men's* bones, and of all uncleanness. Even so ye also outwardly appear righteous unto men, but within ye are full of hypocrisy and iniquity. Woe unto you, scribes and Pharisees, hypocrites! because ye build the tombs of the prophets, and garnish the sepulchres of the righteous, And say, If we had been in the days of our fathers, we would not have been partakers with them in the blood of the prophets. Wherefore ye be witnesses unto yourselves, that ye are the children of them which killed the prophets. Fill ye up then the measure of your fathers. *Ye serpents, ye* generation of vipers, how can ye escape the damnation of hell?" (Matt. 23:1–33 KJV).

Jesus admonishes the Pharisees for their pride, selfishness, and hypocritical behavior, and pronounces woes unto them. (A woe is pronouncement of judgment.) I want you to pay close attention to these next verses: they reveal the debt owed.

"Wherefore, behold, I send unto you prophets, and wise men, and scribes: and *some* of them ye shall kill and crucify; and *some* of them shall ye scourge in your synagogues, and persecute *them* from city to city" (Matt. 23:34 KJV).

Jesus said, I send prophets, wise men, and scribes, and some of them ye SHALL kill and crucify. This is just what the Israelites did before they were conquered by the Babylonians. Jesus is speaking of himself, his disciples, and other believers being killed and crucified. What did Jesus say the purpose of the martyrdom and persecution of the believers and his crucifixion was? Pay close attention to the next verse.

"That upon you may come all the righteous blood, shed upon the earth, from the blood of righteous Abel unto the blood of Zacharias son of Barachias, whom ye slew between the temple and the altar" (Matt. 23:35 KJV).

The purpose was to judge Israel for all of the righteous blood shed upon the earth. Jesus is saying that the blood of the murders of all the prophets would be poured out on the generation to whom Jesus was speaking. Why would God wait to judge Israel all those years from the time of Abel until after the time of Jesus? God's forgiveness was received through animal sacrifices, but when Jesus was offered, Israel as a nation rejected him and had to be judged because their sin remained. Before Jesus, God's judgment was stayed because of atonement through sacrifices. After Jesus, the only way to receive a stay of judgment was to accept Jesus as one's savior and ask for the forgiveness of sin. Jesus also specified when this would happen.

"Verily I say unto you, All these things shall come upon this generation"(Matt. 23:36 KJV).

All the righteous blood shed upon the earth was poured out on the generation to whom Jesus was speaking. It happened forty years after Jesus's resurrection, and he even mentions the destruction of Jerusalem.

"*O Jerusalem, Jerusalem, thou that killest the prophets, and stonest them which are sent unto thee,* how often would I have gathered thy children together, even as a hen gathereth her chickens under *her* wings, and ye would not! *Behold, your house is left unto you desolate*" (Matt. 23:37–38 KJV, emphasis mine).

Jesus called Jerusalem desolate! Let me remind you of the Scriptures we have already discussed so that you have the full picture.

"Your *country is desolate, your cities are burned with fire: your land, strangers devour it in your presence, and it is desolate, as overthrown by strangers.* And the daughter of Zion is left as a cottage in a vineyard, as a lodge in a garden of cucumbers, *as a besieged city. Except the LORD of hosts had left unto us a very small remnant, we should have been as Sodom, and we should have been like unto Gomorrah*" (Isaiah 1:7–9 KJV, emphasis mine).

"And when ye spread forth your hands, I will hide mine eyes from you: yea, when ye make many prayers, *I will not hear: your hands are full of blood*" (Isaiah 1:14–15 KJV, emphasis mine).

The judgment would not be delayed because they crucified the Lord and killed and persecuted his followers. God said, I will not hear your prayers. Again, let's confirm this.

"But as for me, my prayer *is* unto thee, O LORD, *in* an acceptable time: O God, in the multitude of thy mercy hear me, in the truth of thy salvation. Deliver me out of the mire, and let me not sink: let me be delivered from them that hate me, and out of the deep waters. Let not the waterflood overflow me, neither let the deep swallow me up, and let not the pit shut her mouth upon me. Hear me, O LORD; for thy lovingkindness *is* good: turn unto me according to the multitude of thy tender mercies. And hide not thy face from thy servant; for I am in trouble: hear me speedily. Draw nigh unto my soul, *and* redeem it: deliver me because of mine enemies. Thou hast known my reproach, and my shame, and my dishonour: mine adversaries *are* all before thee. Reproach hath broken my heart; and I am full of heaviness: and I looked *for some* to take pity, but *there was* none; and for comforters, but I found none. They gave me also gall for my meat; and in my thirst they gave me vinegar to drink"(Psalms 69:13–21 KJV).

Do you remember when Jesus was on the cross and they gave him vinegar to drink when he was thirsty? This is a Messianic psalm. Notice what the next verses say will happen to the unbelievers and religious class of Israel.

"Let their table become a snare before them: and *that which should have been* for *their* welfare, *let it become* a trap. Let their eyes be darkened, that they see not; and make their loins continually to shake. *Pour out thine indignation upon them*, and let thy wrathful anger take hold of them. *Let their habitation be desolate; and* let none dwell in their tents. For they persecute *him* whom thou hast smitten; and they talk to the grief of those whom thou hast wounded. *Add iniquity unto their iniquity*: and let them not come into thy righteousness. Let them be blotted out of the book of the living, and not be written with the righteous" (Psalms 69:22–28 KJV, emphasis mine).

God says to "add iniquity unto their iniquity." What does he mean here? He is speaking about all the righteous blood shed upon the earth, being poured out upon the generation that crucified Jesus. Now, we see what "that determined shall be poured upon the desolate" means. It is all the righteous blood shed upon the earth and poured upon the desolate, which refers to Jerusalem.

"And he shall confirm the covenant with many for one week: and in the midst of the week he shall cause the sacrifice and the oblation to cease, and for the overspreading of abominations he shall make it desolate, even until the consummation, and that determined shall be poured upon the desolate*"* (Dan. 9:27 KJV, emphasis mine).

Can you see the picture that is being formed? One difficult aspect in understanding a prophecy is discovering an actual time or date for its fulfillment. There has been much debate over the book of Revelation and the date when it was written. The consensus is that it was written around 96 A.D. In the past, I was not concerned with this matter, and I had no reason to debate it. After seeking understanding of the book of Revelation, I have found some very interesting information that defies accepted opinion. One obvious problem I discovered is that the fulfillment could not have occurred before the prophecy was received, and some events in Revelation occurred during 70 A.D. or possibly just prior. Let's move on from the revelation of the martyr's blood being poured out on Israel and find out how it relates to the book of Revelation.

"Wherefore, behold, I send unto you prophets, and wise men, and scribes: and *some* of them ye shall kill and crucify; and *some* of them shall ye scourge in your synagogues, and persecute *them* from city to city: That upon you may come all the righteous blood shed upon the earth, from the blood of righteous Abel unto the blood of Zacharias son of Barachias, whom ye slew between the temple and the altar. Verily I say unto you, All these things shall come upon this generation. O Jerusalem, Jerusalem, *thou* that killest the prophets, and stonest them which are sent unto thee, how often would I have gathered thy children together, even as a hen gathereth her chickens under *her* wings, and ye would not! Behold, your house is left unto you desolate" (Matt. 23:34–38 KJV).

I have done an extensive study of this set of Scriptures in Matthew 23. We have learned that Jesus was speaking to the Pharisees about how they killed, crucified, scourged, and persecuted prophets, wise men, and scribes. The reason Jesus gave was that all the righteous blood shed upon the earth would come upon them (the Pharisees and Jerusalem). Jesus was pronouncing judgment upon them for an appointed time. We also know that this occurred in 70 A.D., with the destruction of the temple and Jerusalem. Again, Jesus said:

"Verily I say unto you, All these things shall come upon this generation. O Jerusalem, Jerusalem, *thou* that killest the prophets, and stonest them which are sent unto thee, how often would I have gathered thy children together, even as a hen gathereth her chickens under *her* wings, and ye would not! Behold, your house is left unto you desolate" (Matt. 23:36–38 KJV).

Verse 37 links the two events together: Jerusalem, *thou* that kills the prophets, and stones them which are sent unto thee. Jesus also explains why Jerusalem had to be destroyed.

"The same day there came certain of the Pharisees, saying unto him, Get thee out, and depart hence: for Herod will kill thee. And he said unto them, Go ye, and tell that fox, Behold, I cast out devils, and I do cures to day and to morrow, and the third *day* I shall be perfected. Nevertheless I must walk to day, and to morrow, and the *day* following: *for it cannot be that a prophet perish out of Jerusalem*" (Luke 13:31–33 KJV, emphasis mine).

The reason Jerusalem had to be destroyed along with the temple is that all of the prophets were martyred in Jerusalem. Luke records the event a little differently than Matthew, which gives us an important link to the book of Revelation.

"And as they led him away, they laid hold upon one Simon, a Cyrenian, coming out of the country, and on him they laid the cross, that he might bear *it* after Jesus. And there followed him a great company of people, and of women, which also bewailed and lamented him. But Jesus turning unto them said, Daughters of Jerusalem, weep not for me, but weep for yourselves, and for your children. For, behold, the days are coming, in the which they shall say, Blessed *are* the barren, and the wombs that never bare, and the paps which never gave suck. Then shall they begin to say to the mountains, Fall on us; and to the hills, Cover us. For if they do these things in a green tree, what shall be done in the dry?" (Luke 23:26–31 KJV).

Jesus tells us exactly who this judgment will affect. The daughters of *Jerusalem* and their children were the ones who would feel the wrath of this judgment. This is another way of saying that Jerusalem would be judged in that generation. This sounds familiar, doesn't it? If we can find this event in the book of Revelation, it proves that the book was written before 70 A.D.

"And when he had opened the fifth seal, I saw under the *altar the souls of them that were slain for the word of God,* and for the testimony which they held: And they cried with a loud voice, saying, *How long, O Lord, holy and true, dost thou not judge and avenge our blood on them that dwell on the earth?* And white robes were given unto every one of them; and it was said unto them, *that they should rest yet for a little season, until their fellowservants also and their brethren, that should be killed as they were, should be fulfilled"* (Rev. 6:9–11 KJV, emphasis mine).

Under the altar were the souls of those who were slain for the Word of God and their testimony. This sounds, to me, like they were martyrs. Notice what they said. How long? How long do you NOT judge and avenge our blood on them that dwell on the earth? It sounds like the martyrs had been waiting a long time for God to judge and avenge their blood. Do you remember Abel's blood?

"And the LORD said unto Cain, Where *is* Abel thy brother? And he said, I know not: *Am* I my brother's keeper? And he said, What hast thou done? *the voice of thy brother's blood crieth unto me from the ground"* (Gen. 4:9–10 KJV, emphasis mine).

What was Abel's blood crying out for? Justice. Abel's blood had been crying out for justice from the time of his murder until the time this prophecy was written. That's a long time to wait. Do you think the martyrs in Revelation are the same ones Jesus spoke of in Matthew 23:35? You guessed it! The fifth seal is yet another warning that the iniquity of the past would be poured upon that generation.

According to Luke, what would that generation and the daughters of Jerusalem say?

"Then shall they begin to say to the mountains, Fall on us; and to the hills, Cover us. For if they do these things in a green tree, what shall be done in the dry?" (Luke 23:29–31 KJV).

That sounds a lot like the opening of the sixth seal. I wonder if they are the same.

"And I beheld when he had opened the sixth seal, and, lo, there was a great earthquake; and the sun became black as sackcloth of hair, and the moon became as blood; And the stars of heaven fell unto the earth, even as a fig tree casteth her untimely figs, when she is shaken of a mighty wind. And the heaven departed as a scroll when it is rolled together; and every mountain and island were moved out of their places. And the kings of the earth, and the great men, and the rich men, and the chief captains, and the mighty men, and every bondman, and every free man, hid themselves in the dens and in the rocks of the mountains; *And said to the mountains and rocks, Fall on us, and hide us from the face of him that sitteth on the throne, and from the wrath of the Lamb: For the great day of his wrath is come; and who shall be able to stand?*" (Rev. 6:12–17 KJV, emphasis mine).

Now you understand what the great day of his wrath is. It's the wrath of God visited on Jerusalem and the temple. These judgments are not executed upon the whole earth, but only on Israel. This is the Wrath of the Lamb. Jesus warns of this wrath and "the end" in the book of Luke.

"*And when ye shall see Jerusalem compassed with armies, then know that the desolation thereof is nigh.* Then let them which are in Judaea flee to the mountains; and let them which are in the midst of it depart out; and let not them that are in the countries enter thereinto. *For these be the days of vengeance, that all things which are written may be fulfilled*" (Luke 21:20–22 KJV, emphasis mine).

Jesus told the daughters of Jerusalem that they would say it would be a blessing to never have children because of the wrath coming to Jerusalem. Now, read the next verse.

"But woe unto them that are with child, and to them that give suck, in those days! for there shall be great distress in the land, and *wrath upon this people*" (Luke 21:23 KJV, emphasis mine).

"And they shall fall by the edge of the sword, and shall be led away captive into all nations: and Jerusalem shall be trodden down of the Gentiles, until the times of the Gentiles be fulfilled" (Luke 21:24 KJV).

Let me connect the next verse in Luke back to the sixth seal, because they refer to the same event.

"And there shall be *signs in the sun, and in the moon, and in the stars*; and upon the earth distress of nations, with perplexity; the sea and the waves roaring" (Luke 21:25 KJV, emphasis mine).

"And I beheld when he had opened the sixth seal, and, lo, there was a great earthquake; and *the sun* became black as sackcloth of hair, and *the moon* became as blood; And the *stars of heaven* fell unto the earth" (Rev. 6:12–13 KJV, emphasis mine).

I challenge you to compare these Scriptures and see for yourself whether they are speaking of the same event. If they are the same event, this means the book of Revelation was written before 70 A.D., or else it would not be useful as a warning to the readers of John.

Chapter 6

———————— 6 ————————

PURPOSE OF THE FULFILLED SEVENTY WEEKS

WE HAVE USED PATTERN AND types and shadows to discover and learn the true interpretation of the seventy weeks of Daniel. We have found that the seventy weeks started at the command to rebuild and restore Jerusalem and ended with the resurrection of Jesus. The final prediction in the prophecy shows the second destruction of Jerusalem and the temple. We have clearly seen this through the type and shadow of Moses and the children of Israel in the wilderness. That generation rejected Moses's direction, and thus rejected God. They died in the wilderness during a forty-year time period. The children of Israel rejected Jesus as the Messiah, and therefore they rejected God. Remember that Jesus said:

"He that hateth me hateth my Father also" (John 15:23 KJV).

That generation also died in the wilderness—the wilderness of unbelief. They literally died at the end of a forty-year period, just as in Moses's day.

We also have seen how the pattern of the number 490 shows the same thing. Jesus warned Israel many times about the impending danger looming over that generation, but they were blind and could not comprehend the truth.

Let's go from here to the purpose of the seventy weeks prophecy.

"Seventy weeks are determined upon thy people and upon thy holy city, to finish the transgression, and to make an end of sins, and to make reconciliation for iniquity, and to bring in everlasting righteousness, and to seal up the vision and prophecy, and to anoint the most Holy" (Dan. 9:24 KJV).

There are six things that the prophecy was to accomplish at its fulfillment:

1. Finish the transgression,
2. Make an end of sins,
3. Make reconciliation for iniquity,
4. Bring in everlasting righteousness,
5. Seal up the vision and prophecy,
6. Anoint the most holy.

Finish the Transgression

The transgression mentioned here is not just sin in the world. If you notice, it's called "the transgression." The book of Daniel has several visions and prophecies that speak of the same event. It tells of the four kingdoms that would rise to power on the earth, indicating the time when the kingdom of God would arise at the end. We can gain an idea of what "the transgression" is from the previous prophecies.

"And it waxed great, *even* to the host of heaven; and it cast down *some* of the host and of the stars to the ground, and stamped upon them. Yea, he magnified *himself* even to the prince of the host, and by him the daily *sacrifice* was taken away, and the place of his sanctuary was cast down. And an host was given *him* against *the daily sacrifice by reason of transgression*, and it cast down the truth to the ground; and it practised, and prospered. Then I heard one saint speaking, and another saint said unto that certain *saint* which spake, How long *shall be* the vision *concerning* the daily *sacrifice, and the transgression of desolation*, to give both the sanctuary and the host to be trodden under foot? And he said unto me, Unto two thousand and three hundred days; then shall the sanctuary be cleansed" (Dan. 8:10–14 KJV, emphasis mine).

In this passage, it is called the transgression of desolation because it is given for the sanctuary and the host to be trodden under foot. The sanctuary was the Jewish temple in which the daily sacrifices were made.

"The transgression" is tied to the destruction of the temple; therefore, it was finished in 70 A.D. when the Romans ransacked Jerusalem and the sanctuary. What was the actual transgression? It was the rejection of Jesus. That is what started the destruction or "desolation." We will discuss this in much more detail in the next chapter. The important point is that "the transgression" was finished in 70 A.D.

MAKE AN END OF SINS—MAKE RECONCILIATION FOR INIQUITY

Both of these concern general sin, meaning the problem of sin itself, rather than something specific. Remember that most prophecy teachers assume this has not come to pass because sin is still present in the world.

"Therefore if any man *be* in Christ, *he is* a new creature: old things are passed away; behold, *all things are become new.* And all things *are* of God, who hath reconciled us to himself by Jesus Christ, and hath given to us the ministry of reconciliation; To wit, that God was in Christ, *reconciling the world unto himself*, not imputing their trespasses unto them; and hath committed unto us the word of reconciliation. Now then we are ambassadors for Christ, as though God did beseech *you* by us: we pray *you* in Christ's stead, *be ye reconciled to God*" (2 Cor. 5:17–20 KJV, emphasis mine).

According to this Scripture, God has already reconciled the whole world unto himself, not imputing their trespasses unto them, and hath committed unto us the word of reconciliation.

"But God commendeth his love toward us, in that, while we were yet sinners, Christ died for us. Much more then, being now justified by his blood, we shall be saved from wrath through him. For if, when we were enemies, *we were reconciled to God by the death of his Son*, much more, being reconciled, we shall be saved by his life" (Romans 5:8–10 KJV, emphasis mine).

God has made end of sin for those who choose Jesus. Think of it this way: if a marriage is reconciled, what has happened? The husband and wife have ceased being separated and become one again. Sin is a separation from God. If we have been reconciled with God, we are no longer separated from him. If you reconcile your checkbook with your bank statement, it means that the balances match. If you are reconciled to Christ, your balance of sin matches his: zero!

"For if we have been planted together in the likeness of his death, we shall be also *in the likeness of his* resurrection: *Knowing this, that our old man is crucified with him, that the body of sin might be destroyed*, that henceforth we should not serve sin. For he that is dead is freed from sin. Now if we be dead with Christ, we believe that we shall also live with him" (Romans 6:4–8 KJV, emphasis mine).

Why was the old man crucified with Jesus. He was crucified with Jesus in order that the body of sin might be destroyed! Does that mean the ability to choose sin has been taken away? No. He says that henceforth we should not serve sin any longer. The choice to sin or not is still there, but the body of sin has been destroyed. God is not going to do anything else about sin because Jesus's sacrifice was enough!

"For then must he often have suffered since the foundation of the world: but now once in the end of the *world hath he appeared to put away sin by the sacrifice of himself*" (Heb. 9:26 KJV, emphasis mine).

This clearly says, Jesus appeared to put away sin by his sacrifice, and that is exactly what he did. The whole point of Jesus's arrival was to make an end of sin.

BRING IN EVERLASTING RIGHTEOUSNESS

What about everlasting righteousness? Did Jesus bring it in?

"For he hath made him *to be* sin for us, who knew no sin; *that we might be made the righteousness of God in him*" (2 Cor. 5:21 KJV, emphasis mine).

"For the kingdom of God is not meat and drink; but *righteousness*, and peace, and joy in the Holy Ghost" (Romans 14:17 KJV, emphasis mine).

"For with the heart man *believeth unto righteousness*; and with the mouth confession is made unto salvation. For the Scripture saith, Whosoever believeth on him shall not be ashamed" (Romans 10:10–11 KJV, emphasis mine).

"That no flesh should glory in his presence. But of him are ye in Christ Jesus, who of God is made unto us wisdom, and *righteousness*, and sanctification, and redemption" (1 Cor. 1:29–30 KJV, emphasis mine).

Jesus Christ has made unto us righteousness! Will Jesus Christ ever be moved, removed, or taken from us? No! He is our everlasting righteousness. When Jesus destroyed the body of sin, righteousness was established because he exchanged our sin for his righteousness.

Seal Up the Vision and Prophecy

What about sealing up the vision and the prophecy? The word "seal" in Hebrew means "to close up" or "make an end to." Jesus's crucifixion sealed up the vision and prophecy of Daniel. He destroyed the body of sin, brought in everlasting righteousness, and set judgment in motion for the Jews who refused Jesus.

"And I heard the man clothed in linen, which *was* upon the waters of the river, when he held up his right hand and his left hand unto heaven, and sware by him that liveth for ever that *it shall be* for a time, times, and an half; *and when he shall have accomplished to scatter the power of the holy people, all these things shall be finished*" (Dan. 12:7 KJV, emphasis mine).

When the holy people were scattered, all these things shall be finished. The holy people (the Jews) were scattered forty years after Jesus's resurrection. This means that the prophecy of the seventy weeks was completely fulfilled in 70 A.D.

Anoint the Most Holy

To "anoint the Most Holy" refers to the anointing of the Messiah. This is very easy to see. Jesus was anointed four different times:

1. At his baptism,
2. Just before his death,
3. After his death, and
4. At his resurrection (he was given a glorified or anointed body).

A great deal could be said about all of these things, but I simply wanted to show that they have all come to pass.

Chapter 7

7

THE MISSING CONTEXT REVEALED

Isn't it great to watch a historical movie? Movies with a true historical background are awesome to me. Even a fictional movie with a true historical time period weaved into the plot is fascinating, but what if you didn't understand anything about the time period or the culture presented in the movie? Most likely, much of the movie would be puzzling to you. The same is true of Scripture. When someone chooses a few verses and does not investigate the context or previous writings, the verses can be confusing. It's as if you started watching a movie in the middle and expected to understand the whole plot. That would not work.

In the many sermons I have heard about Mathew 24, I have never heard anyone explain the previous chapter or make connections between the two. That's one reason those interpretations were incorrect. Most preachers and teachers take the whole chapter of Matthew chapter 24 out of it original context and discuss it alone.

In order to understand the setting for Matthew 24, let's read chapter 23.

"Then spake Jesus to the multitude, and to his disciples, Saying, The scribes and the Pharisees sit in Moses' seat: All therefore whatsoever they bid you observe, *that* observe and do; but do not ye after their works: for they say, and do not. For they bind heavy burdens and grievous to be borne, and lay *them* on men's shoulders; but they *themselves* will not move them with one of their fingers. But all their works they do for to be seen of men: they make broad their phylacteries, and enlarge the borders of their garments, And love the uppermost rooms at feasts, and the chief seats in the synagogues, And greetings in the markets, and to be called of men, Rabbi, Rabbi. But be not ye called Rabbi: for one is your Master, *even* Christ; and all ye are brethren. And call no *man* your father upon the earth: for one is your Father, which is in heaven. Neither be ye called masters: for one is your Master, *even* Christ. But he that is greatest among you shall be your servant. *And whosoever shall exalt himself shall be abased; and he that shall humble himself shall be exalted*" (Matt. 23:1–12 KJV, emphasis mine).

Notice how Jesus is exposing those who have the intent to murder him. He prophesied in verse 12 that the Pharisees would be cast down or abased. Pride exalts itself. You begin to see the context for the next chapter here. Jesus is confronting the Pharisees and telling them directly that they will be abased.

"But woe unto you, scribes and Pharisees, hypocrites! for ye shut up the kingdom of heaven against men: for ye neither go in *yourselves*, neither suffer ye them that are entering to go in. Woe unto you, scribes and Pharisees, hypocrites! for ye devour widows' houses, and for a pretence make long prayer: therefore ye shall receive the greater damnation. Woe unto you, scribes and Pharisees, hypocrites! for ye compass sea and land to make one proselyte, and when he is made, ye make him twofold more the child of hell than yourselves. Woe unto you, *ye* blind guides, which say, Whosoever shall swear by the temple, it is nothing; but whosoever shall swear by the gold of the temple, he is a debtor! *Ye* fools and blind: for whether is greater, the gold, or the temple that sanctifieth the gold? And, Whosoever shall swear by the altar, it is nothing; but whosoever sweareth by the gift that is upon it, he is guilty. *Ye* fools and blind: for whether *is* greater, the gift, or the altar that sanctifieth the gift? Whoso therefore shall swear by the altar, sweareth by it, and by all things thereon. And whoso shall swear by the temple, sweareth by it, and by him that dwelleth therein. And he that shall swear by heaven, sweareth by the throne of God, and by him that sitteth thereon. Woe unto you, scribes and Pharisees, hypocrites! for ye pay tithe of mint and anise and cummin, and have omitted the weightier *matters* of the law, judgment, mercy, and faith: these ought ye to have done, and not to leave the other undone. *Ye* blind guides, which strain at a gnat, and swallow a camel. Woe unto you, scribes and Pharisees, hypocrites! for ye make clean the outside of the cup and of the platter, but within they are full of extortion and excess. *Thou* blind Pharisee, cleanse first that *which is* within the cup and platter, that the outside of them may be clean also. Woe unto you, scribes and Pharisees, hypocrites! for ye are like unto whited sepulchres, which indeed appear beautiful outward, but are within full of dead *men's* bones, and of all uncleanness. Even so ye also outwardly appear righteous unto men, but within ye are full of hypocrisy and iniquity" (Matt. 23:13–28 KJV).

Jesus didn't cut them any slack, did he? Can you imagine how angry this made the Pharisees and Scribes?

Jesus pronounces "woes" unto them. Do you remember the woes pronounced upon people and cities in the Old Testament? These were judgments from God himself. The Pharisees knew this, and Jesus was pronouncing woes upon them just like in the Old Testament. Jesus goes into greater detail in the next few verses.

"Woe unto you, scribes and Pharisees, hypocrites! because ye build the tombs of the prophets, and garnish the sepulchres of the righteous, And say, If we had been in the days of our fathers, we would not have been partakers with them in the blood of the prophets. Wherefore ye be witnesses unto yourselves, that ye are the children of them which killed the prophets" (Matt. 23:29–31 KJV).

Jesus is basically saying that the blood of the prophets was on the Pharisees' hands. What an accusation!

"Fill ye up then the measure of your fathers" (Matt. 23:32 KJV).

In other words, he was saying they will do the exact same thing as their fathers, whether they be martyr prophets, wise men, or scribes.

"*Ye* serpents, *ye* generation of vipers, how can ye escape the damnation of hell? Wherefore, behold, I send unto you *prophets, and wise men, and scribes: and some of them ye shall kill and crucify; and some of them shall ye scourge in your synagogues, and persecute them from city to city*"(Matt. 23:33–34 KJV emphasis mine).

Jesus is prophesying that the Pharisees would do exactly the same things as their fathers! He is speaking of his crucifixion, the persecution of his disciples, and the martyrdom of believers in the near future. Jesus also gives the results of the vicious acts against God.

"*That upon you may come all the righteous blood shed upon the earth*, from the blood of righteous Abel unto the blood of Zacharias son of Barachias, whom ye slew between the temple and the altar" (Matt. 23:35 KJV, emphasis mine).

Did you understand that? The crucifixion of Jesus and the murder and persecution of believers would cause all the righteous blood shed upon the earth to be on the Pharisees hands. They would be judged for the murder of these martyrs. Jesus then gives the time period in which this judgment would occur.

"Verily I say unto you, All these things shall come upon this generation" (Matt. 23:36 KJV, emphasis mine).

These things would happen to the generation to whom Jesus was speaking. This is not something that will occur during a later generation, such as ours. Jesus also discloses the location of this event.

"O Jerusalem, Jerusalem, *thou* that killest the prophets, and stonest them which are sent unto thee, how often would I have gathered thy children together, even as a hen gathereth her chickens under *her* wings, and ye would not! Behold, your house is left unto you desolate. For I say unto you, Ye shall not see me henceforth, till ye shall say, Blessed *is* he that cometh in the name of the Lord" (Matt. 23:37–39 KJV, emphasis mine).

Jerusalem is the location where these events would happen. Jesus says that Jerusalem figuratively killed the prophets, meaning that it was the place where the prophets were killed.

Now put yourself in the place of the disciples at this time. You are hearing about all the things that are going to come to pass, and none of it sounds good. What would be your first question? When are all these things going to happen? That's what I would be wondering. The disciples were human just like you and I, and they responded in the same way.

"And Jesus went out, and departed from the temple: and his disciples came to *him* for to shew him the buildings of the temple. And Jesus said unto them, See ye not all these things? verily I say unto you, There shall not be left here one stone upon another, that shall not be thrown down. And as he sat upon the mount of Olives, the disciples came unto him privately, saying, Tell us, *when shall these things be? and what shall be the sign of thy coming, and of the end of the world?*" (Matt. 24:1–3 KJV, emphasis mine).

As soon as they could ask Jesus privately, they said, "Tell us, when shall these things be?" What things were these? The blood of the prophets being poured out on that generation, the destruction of the temple (verse 2), and the persecution of which Jesus spoke. You have to remember that Jesus's death and resurrection were mysterious to the disciples. All these other things were certainly mysteries as well.

In the minds of the disciples, the mission of the Messiah was much different than Jesus's actual actions. They fought over who was going to be on the right hand and the left in his kingdom. Why? The teaching of the day was that the Messiah would come and make Israel the head and not the tail. They believed that he would end the Roman occupation of Israel and the Jews would rule the world in an earthly kingdom that would never end. The Messiah would rule with a rod of iron and carry the government on his shoulders. This is also the reason why the religious leaders did not recognize Jesus as Messiah. Jesus did not fit their mold. It was this belief about the Messiah that led to Israel's total destruction in 70 A.D. The leaders rejected the true Messiah, and therefore, they were still waiting for the Messiah to come. This strong delusion resulted in their continued search for a leader to appear and remove the Romans. It wasn't long before someone else declared himself the Messiah and tried to defeat the Romans, with terrible results. False prophets prophesied to Israel, giving the people false hope about defeating the Roman occupation, when all the time the Scriptures predicted quite the opposite. If Israel had not tried to rise up against the Romans, Jerusalem and the temple would not have been destroyed. The Romans grew tired of the constant uprisings, so they decided to destroy Israel's city, temple, and way of life, and then scatter the people so that they would not have a large enough group in one place to cause trouble again. This was the complete fulfillment of the prophecy of the seventy weeks.

Matthew 24 explains the judgments that were pronounced in chapter 23 and proclaimed by Jesus as occurring in the generation to whom he was speaking. All these events happened in the context of Scripture and history, which helps us to understand them more fully.

Chapter 8

8

JESUS WARNS OF
IMMINENT JUDGMENT

ONE OF THE DIFFICULT ASPECTS in interpreting prophecy is discovering
the correct time period for its fulfillment. In order for an interpretation
to be accurate, the time period has to be confirmed absolutely. A great rule
to remember is that the whole of Scripture revolves around Jesus and his
first coming, so this should be the first time period considered for the
fulfillment of a prophecy. Matthew 24 has been viewed as a future prophecy.
However, if this prophecy has not yet been fulfilled, then there is no way
to confirm when it will take place except for the "signs of the times," which
are favored in so many sermons. These signs, which include floods, famines,
earthquakes, wars, and the whole world generally going to Hell fast and
furiously, have been happening for many, many years. Doesn't it make sense
that Jesus would refer to a particular set of clear signs? In this chapter,
we will discover what Jesus was warning the disciples about, and what
particular signs he was talking about.

"And Jesus went out, and departed from the temple: and his disciples
came to *him* for to shew him the buildings of the temple. And Jesus said
unto them, See ye not all these things? verily I say unto you, There shall not
be left here one stone upon another, that shall not be thrown down. And
as he sat upon the mount of Olives, the disciples came unto him privately,

saying, Tell us, when shall these things be? and what *shall be* the sign of thy coming, and of the end of the world?" (Matt. 24:1–3 KJV).

Do you remember the context? Jesus had just finished telling the Pharisees that the blood of all the murdered prophets would be poured out on that generation. Afterward, when they went outside, the disciples pointed out the buildings and the temple to Jesus. Jesus responded by saying, "there shall not be left here one stone upon another that shall not be thrown down." Jesus is indicating that all of those buildings would be completely leveled. The disciples asked him when this would happen and what the signs were for his coming and for the end of the world. Apparently, Jesus mentioned not only the destruction of the temple and the blood of the prophets being poured out, but also his coming and the end of the world. It's curious that the second coming of Christ is not mentioned in Jesus's comments to the Pharisees. The destruction of the temple and the end of the system of sacrifice would be like the end of the world for the Jews. We will discuss this in detail as we progress.

"And Jesus answered and said unto them, Take heed that no man deceive you. For many shall come in my name, saying, I am Christ; and shall deceive many" (Matt. 24:4–5 KJV).

Here, Jesus is beginning to answer the questions of his disciples. We have to first determine a time of fulfillment for Jesus's statements. Remember, he is referring to what would be poured out on the Pharisees of that generation, so we must seek to understand the deception that Jesus is warning the disciples about. Deceptions have existed since the beginning of time. What deception is Jesus speaking of? Verse 5 gives us the answer, "many shall come in my name saying, I AM CHRIST." This could have started only during the time of Jesus because that was when the Messiah had been predicted by Scripture to appear. Who were the ones who were going to see this happen? The disciples were. Remember that Jesus said the blood of the prophets would be poured out on *that generation*. The disciples asked when these things would occur, and he gave *them* signs to look for. Jesus warned the disciples that many would come and say that they were the Christ. Why would this deceive the disciples so easily? Jesus knew that they would not understand his death on the cross, and that they would forsake him. They would question everything. Why? The accepted theology about the purpose of the Messiah (false doctrine) would lead them and all of Israel down the wrong path. Do you remember how they kept asking Jesus who among them would hold positions of authority in the kingdom of God? They expected that since they had found the Messiah and become his disciples, they would rule at the top with him. All of Israel expected the Messiah to come and throw off Roman oppression, so that Israel would again be the head, rather than the tail, as in the days of King David. The Messiah would rule with a rod of iron and the government would rest upon his shoulders. This was the main mission of the Messiah, according to Jewish beliefs at the time. But, Jesus did not do what they expected. This was confusing to the disciples after Jesus's death. And, after Jesus was raised from the dead, the disciples questioned him.

"And, being assembled together with *them*, commanded them that they should not depart from Jerusalem, but wait for the promise of the Father, which, *saith he*, ye have heard of me. For John truly baptized with water; but ye shall be baptized with the Holy Ghost not many days hence.

When they therefore were come together, they asked of him, saying, *Lord, wilt thou at this time restore again the kingdom to Israel?*" (Acts 1:3–6 KJV, emphasis mine).

Even then, the disciples were expecting the oppression of the Romans to be removed. Jesus tells them not to be deceived because others will come, using his name and claiming to be the Christ. This means that those pretending to be Christ would try to lead a revolution against the Roman occupation. That is exactly what happened; many claimed to be the Messiah and led a rebellion against the Roman Empire. This is what caused the Romans to utterly destroy Jerusalem, which makes perfect sense. Israel, for the most part, rejected Jesus as Messiah, so they were still looking for the promised one to come and break with the Romans. This explains why Jesus said, "shall deceive many." This is a very important point!

"And ye shall hear of wars and rumours of wars: see that ye be not troubled: for all *these things* must come to pass, but the end is not yet" (Matt. 24:6 KJV).

Jesus also mentions wars and rumors of wars. Again, wars have existed for a very long time, so he must be pointing out something in particular.

These wars and rumors of wars were started by the Jews who rejected Jesus and were trying to fight the Romans. Remember that this is what the Jews thought the Messiah's mission would be. Each time a false Messiah appeared, they led a rebellion against the Romans. Jesus said these things must come to pass. Why? The constant uprisings of the false messiahs convinced the Romans to finally put an end to the tiresome Jews. This was prophesied beforehand and had to come to pass.

Many preachers today use this Scripture to prove that the end times are filled with wars and rumors of wars. These good men of God rationalize that the end has not come, so this Scripture has not been fulfilled. Therefore, they look for these wars and rumors of wars in our time. It's an understandable position, but the context shows that the disciples were going to see these things, not us. Later in this study, I will elaborate on the nature of the end.

"For nation shall rise against nation, and kingdom against kingdom: and there shall be famines, and pestilences, and earthquakes, in diverse places. All these *are* the beginning of sorrows" (Matt. 24:7–8 KJV).

Where did this eschatology come from? Was this a new revelation that Jesus had just received from the Father? No. There are patterns of these things in Scripture. Let's look at one such pattern.

In the book of Jeremiah, Israel was in rebellion against God, and they began to worship other gods and follow false prophets. God tried to warn Israel many times through the prophets, but they refused to listen, and judgment was going to fall upon Israel for their disobedience. This is the context for the next Scripture.

"In the beginning of the reign of Jehoiakim the son of Josiah king of Judah came this word unto Jeremiah from the LORD, saying, Thus saith the LORD to me; Make thee bonds and yokes, and put them upon thy neck, And send them to the king of Edom, and to the king of Moab, and to the king of the Ammonites, and to the king of Tyrus, and to the king of Zidon, by the hand of the messengers which come to Jerusalem unto Zedekiah king of Judah; And command them to say unto their masters, Thus saith the LORD of hosts, the God of Israel; Thus shall ye say unto your masters; I have made the earth, the man and the beast that *are* upon the ground, by my great power and by my outstretched arm, and have given it unto whom it seemed meet unto me. And now have I given all these lands into the hand of Nebuchadnezzar the king of Babylon, my servant; and the beasts of the field have I given him also to serve him. And all nations shall serve him, and his son, and his son's son, until the very time of his land come: and then many nations and great kings shall serve themselves of him. And it shall come to pass, *that* the nation and kingdom which will not serve the same Nebuchadnezzar the king of Babylon, and that will not put their neck under the yoke of the king of Babylon, that nation will I punish, saith the LORD, with the sword, and with the famine, and with the pestilence, until I have consumed them by his hand. Therefore hearken not ye to your prophets, nor to your diviners, nor to your dreamers, nor to your enchanters, nor to your sorcerers, which speak unto you, saying, Ye shall not serve the king of Babylon: For they prophesy a lie unto you, to remove you far from your land; and that I should drive you out, and ye should perish. But the nations that bring their neck under the yoke of the king of Babylon, and serve him, those will I let remain still in their own land, saith the LORD; and they shall till it, and dwell therein" (Jer. 27:1–11 KJV).

Jeremiah prophesied to Israel that they would be ruled over by the king of Babylon. Israel would not repent, so God had to punish them, and this was God's judgment for their disobedience. Notice in verse 8 that whoever would not submit to Babylon would be punished with the sword, with famine, and with pestilence. Through Jeremiah, God also warns Israel not to listen to prophets who prophesy that they would overcome the king of Babylon. If they resisted, God would scatter them throughout the world.

Here, we have false prophets with a false word from God, wars and rumors of wars, nation against nation, famines, and pestilences. These are the exact things Jesus is talking about in Matthew. This is a type and shadow of what would happen in Jesus's time. Jeremiah prophesied that the king of Babylon would take control, and Ezekiel predicted the fall of Jerusalem and the temple. False prophets continually told the people that God would not allow this to happen, but Jerusalem and the temple ended up being destroyed and the people of Israel were scattered throughout the world at that time. In Matthew 24, Jesus warns the Jews of his day about the same thing. The difference is that the Romans would be the nation who destroyed

Jerusalem and the temple. Many false Messiahs came and prophesied that God wanted the Jews to fight the Romans and that the Messiah would lead them to victory. The Jews were then destroyed by the sword, famine (because the Romans cut off their food supply), and pestilences. If you check the history of this time period, there were earthquakes during and just after the fall of Jerusalem.

This was a warning to the disciples of what would come and what they would experience. With every rejection of Jesus, Israel experienced a greater falling away from God. And, during Paul's later missionary journeys, many people who believed in Jesus left the faith because of false Messiahs. In fact, many of Paul's letters are an encouragement to keep faith. The book of Hebrews described the Jewish people turning away from faith in Jesus and back to the law. Israel had rejected their Messiah, and judgment would fall upon them, just as in the days of Jeremiah. Jerusalem and the temple would be destroyed once again, and the Jewish people would be scattered throughout the nations once more.

Let us dig a bit deeper. Jesus said that that these events would be the "beginning of sorrows." Sorrows are a reference to birth, and again, Jesus is referencing Scripture. The book of Isaiah was written before the Babylonian invasion as well, and in it, Isaiah conveys God's warnings to the Israelites. As we have seen, these warnings also apply to Israel during the time of Jesus. Isaiah 66 gives one such warning.

"Thus saith the LORD, The heaven *is* my throne, and the earth *is* my footstool: where *is* the house that ye build unto me? and where *is* the place of my rest? For all those *things* hath mine hand made, and all those *things* have been, saith the LORD: but to this *man* will I look, *even to him that is* poor and of a contrite spirit, and trembleth at my word. He that killeth an ox *is as if* he slew a man; he that sacrificeth a lamb, *as if* he cut off a dog's neck; he that offereth an oblation, *as if he offered* swine's blood; he that burneth incense, *as if* he blessed an idol. Yea, they have chosen their own ways, and their soul delighteth in their abominations. *I also will choose their delusions, and will bring their fears upon them; because when I called, none did answer; when I spake, they did not hear*: but they did evil before mine eyes, and chose *that* in which I delighted not.

Hear the word of the LORD, ye that tremble at his word; *Your brethren that hated you, that cast you out for my name's sake*, said, Let the LORD be glorified: but he shall appear to your joy, and they shall be ashamed. A voice of noise from the city, a voice from the temple, a voice of the LORD *that rendereth recompence to his enemies. Before she travailed, she brought forth; before her pain came, she was delivered of a man child.* Who hath heard such a thing? who hath seen such things? Shall the earth be made to bring forth in one day? or shall a nation be born at once? *for as soon as Zion travailed, she brought forth her children. Shall I bring to the birth, and not cause to bring forth?* saith the LORD: shall I cause to bring forth, and shut *the womb?* saith thy God. Rejoice ye with Jerusalem, and be glad with her, all ye that love her: rejoice for joy with her, *all ye that mourn for her:* That ye may suck, and be satisfied with the breasts of her consolations; that ye may milk out, and be delighted with the abundance of her glory. For thus saith the LORD, *Behold, I will extend peace to her like a river, and the glory of the Gentiles like a flowing stream: then shall ye suck, ye shall be borne upon her sides, and be dandled upon her knees.* As one whom his mother comforteth, so will I comfort you; and ye shall be comforted in Jerusalem. And when ye see *this*, your heart shall rejoice, and your bones shall flourish like an herb: and the hand of the LORD shall be known toward his servants, and *his* indignation toward his enemies.

For, behold, the LORD will come with fire, and with his chariots like a whirlwind, to render his anger with fury, and his rebuke with flames of fire. For by fire and by his sword will the LORD plead with all flesh: and the slain of the LORD shall be many. They that sanctify themselves, and purify themselves in the gardens behind one *tree* in the midst, eating swine's flesh, and the abomination, and the mouse, shall be consumed together, saith the LORD. For I *know* their works and their thoughts: it shall come, that I will gather all nations and tongues; and they shall come, and see my glory. And I will set a sign among them, and I will send those that escape of them unto the nations, *to* Tarshish, Pul, and Lud, that draw the bow, *to* Tubal, and Javan, *to* the isles afar off, that have not heard my fame, neither have seen my glory; and they shall declare my glory among the Gentiles. And they shall bring all your brethren *for* an offering unto the LORD out of all nations upon horses, and in chariots, and in litters, and upon mules, and upon swift beasts, to my holy mountain Jerusalem, saith the LORD, as the children of Israel bring an offering in a clean vessel into the of the LORD. And I will also take of them for priests *and* for Levites, saith the LORD. For as the new heavens and the new earth, which I will make, shall remain before me, saith the LORD, so shall your seed and your name remain. And it shall come to pass, *that* from one new moon to another, and from one sabbath to another, shall all flesh come to worship before me, saith the LORD. And they shall go forth, and look upon the carcases of the men that have transgressed against me: for their worm shall not die, neither shall their fire be quenched; and they shall be an abhorring unto all flesh" (Isaiah 66:1–24 KJV, emphasis mine).

Wow, there is a lot of revelation in that! In verses 1–3, God is looking for a contrite spirit who trembles at his word, but what he finds are those who chose their own way, a way that delighted in abominations. In Jesus's day, the Jews chose another Messiah and also chose to continue with the animal sacrifices that were a slap in the face of God and Jesus, an abomination. In verse, 5 God mentions believers being hated and cast out for his sake. The disciples and believers were hated because of the name of Jesus, and God promises joy to the believer, shame to the unbeliever, and recompense to his enemies. Notice that verse 7, though, discusses the sorrows or travails we are studying in Matthew.

"Before she travailed, she brought forth; before her pain came, she was delivered of a man child" (Isaiah 66:7 KJV).

Before the pain of childbirth, she (Israel) was delivered of a man child (Jesus). The pain of the birth came after Jesus died on the cross and was resurrected. Israel was delivered spiritually from their sins before the pain of childbirth, which was the destruction of Jerusalem, the temple, and the scattering of the Jewish people throughout the nations. The contractions of the birth were the false messiahs, wars, rumors of wars, famines, pestilences, and earthquakes.

The question here is what is being birthed? What possibly could have been born out of the destruction of Israel? This is alluded to in the next few verses.

"*Rejoice ye with Jerusalem, and be glad with her, all ye that love her: rejoice for joy with her, all ye that mourn for her: That ye may suck, and be satisfied with the breasts of her consolations*; that ye may milk out, and be delighted with the abundance of her glory. For thus saith the LORD, Behold, I will extend peace to her like a river, and the glory of the Gentiles like a flowing stream: then shall ye suck, ye shall be borne upon *her* sides, and be dandled upon *her* knees. As one whom his mother comforteth, so will I comfort you; and ye shall be comforted in Jerusalem. And when ye see *this*, your heart shall rejoice, and your bones shall flourish like an herb: and the hand of the LORD shall be known toward his servants, and *his* indignation toward his enemies" (Isaiah 66:9–14 KJV, emphasis mine).

When a woman gives birth, she is left exhausted and desolate. Here, Jerusalem is pregnant, gives birth to something in 70 A.D., and is left desolate.

"Hear another parable: There was a certain householder, which planted a vineyard, and hedged it round about, and digged a winepress in it, and built a tower, and let it out to husbandmen, and went into a far country: And when the time of the fruit drew near, he sent his servants to the husbandmen, that they might receive the fruits of it. And the husbandmen took his servants, and beat one, and killed another, and stoned another. Again, he sent other servants more than the first: and they did unto them likewise. But last of all he sent unto them his son, saying, They will reverence my son. But when the husbandmen saw the son, they said among themselves, This is the heir; come, let us kill him, and let us seize on his inheritance. And they caught him, and cast *him* out of the vineyard, and slew *him*. When the lord therefore of the vineyard cometh, what will he do unto those husbandmen? They say unto him, He will miserably destroy those wicked men, and will let out *his* vineyard unto other husbandmen, which shall render him the fruits in their seasons. Jesus saith unto them, Did ye never read in the Scriptures, The stone which the builders rejected, the same is become the head of the corner: this is the Lord's doing, and it is marvellous in our eyes? Therefore say I unto you, *The kingdom of God shall be taken from you, and given to a nation bringing forth the fruits thereof.* And whosoever shall fall on this stone shall be broken: but on whomsoever it shall fall, it will grind him to powder" (Matt. 21:33–44 KJV, emphasis mine).

The birth is the birth of the kingdom of God being taken away from Israel and given to another nation (the Gentile church) that will bring forth its fruits. Let's get back to Matthew 24.

"Then shall they deliver you up to be afflicted, and shall kill you: and ye shall be hated of all nations for my name's sake. And then shall many be offended, and shall betray one another, and shall hate one another. And many false prophets shall rise, and shall deceive many. And because iniquity shall abound, the love of many shall wax cold" (Matt. 24:9–12 KJV).

Jesus explains the circumstances the disciples would face. The hatred from other Jews who refused to accept Jesus as Messiah would be fierce. Rome would hate the Jewish people because of their persistence in fighting them. And, later in history, other nations would hate Israelites for crucifying Jesus (which is silly). Jesus continued, saying that the love of the Jewish people would grow cold. Why? Think about this: Israel had been waiting for their Messiah for many years, and they knew that the time for him to appear was close, so their expectations were high. As time passed and the Messiah did not show up (at least, not the one for whom they were looking), the people began to doubt the Scriptures. The whole subject of God became a joke to many of them because they didn't see the Messiah. Can you imagine the frustration these people must have experienced? All of the tenets the elders had taught and preached about the Messiah didn't come to pass. For years, the stories of how the Messiah would come and set their nation free were passed down, but they missed the true purpose of God. This is what led Peter to later write:

"Knowing this first, that there shall come in the last days scoffers, walking after their own lusts, And saying, Where is the promise of his coming? for since the fathers fell asleep, all things continue as they were from the beginning of the creation. For this they willingly are ignorant of, that by the word of God the heavens were of old, and the earth standing out of the water and in the water: Whereby the world that then was, being overflowed with water, perished: But the heavens and the earth, which are now, by the same

word are kept in store, reserved unto fire against the day of judgment and perdition of ungodly men" (2 Peter 3:3–7 KJV, emphasis mine).

Because they had not recognized the coming of Jesus as Messiah and they were still waiting for his coming, their love for God grows cold, as does their love for other people.

Also, notice that this is supposed to happen in the last days. It did! It occurred in the last days of Israel as a nation, and in the last days of the Old Covenant, as well. The sacrifices made in the temple were stopped, never to be accepted by God again. This was the end of the Old Testament age and system. This provides the context for Peter's message in the book of 2 Peter. When the Bible mentions the last days, it may not refer to the last days of world or the end of time as we know it. We must study the context to determine the meaning.

Now, how did Jesus know that these things would happen? From a prophesy in the Old Testament, which the Pharisees and Scribes had overlooked and misinterpreted. Jesus took the revelation of family members betraying one another from the book of Micah.

The book of Micah was written around the same time as the book of Isaiah. Micah condemns the rulers, priests, and prophets of Israel who exploit and mislead the people, and prophesies that because of their deeds, Jerusalem will be destroyed by Babylon. He also proclaims the deliverance of the people who go from Jerusalem to Babylon and concludes with an exhortation for Jerusalem to destroy the nations gathered against her. The prophet proclaims that the ideal ruler would come from Bethlehem to defend the nation and that the remnant of Jacob will triumph. He also foresees a day when Yahweh will purge the nation of idolatry and reliance on military might. Micah sets forth a powerful and concise summary of Yahweh's requirement for justice and loyalty and pronounces judgment upon those who have followed the ways of Omri and Ahab. The book closes with a prophetic liturgy comprising elements of a lament. Israel confesses its sin and is assured of deliverance through Yahweh's mighty acts.

Read what Micah says would happen to the Israelites of that time and see if you can find how the pattern fits the time of Jesus as well.

"Woe is me! for I am as when they have gathered the summer fruits, as the grapegleanings of the vintage: *there is* no cluster to eat: my soul desired the firstripe fruit. The good *man* is perished out of the earth: and *there is* none upright among men: they all lie in wait for blood; they hunt every man his brother with a net. That they may do evil with both hands earnestly, the prince asketh, and the judge *asketh* for a reward; and the great *man*, he uttereth his mischievous desire: so they wrap it up. The best of them *is* as a brier: the most upright *is sharper* than a thorn hedge: *the day of thy watchmen and thy visitation cometh; now shall be their perplexity. Trust ye not in a friend, put ye not confidence in a guide: keep the doors of thy mouth from her that lieth in thy bosom. For the son dishonoureth the father, the daughter riseth up against her mother, the daughter in law against her mother in law; a man's enemies are the men of his own house*" (Micah 7:1–6 KJV, emphasis mine).

Did you see it? He said the day of visitation (Messiah) shall be their perplexity. Confusion would reign for the majority of the people on the day of visitation. Jesus was aware of this.

"And the Lord said, Who then is that faithful and wise steward, whom *his* lord shall make ruler over his household, to give *them their* portion of meat in due season? Blessed *is* that servant, whom his lord when he cometh shall find so doing. Of a truth I say unto you, that he will make him ruler over all that he hath. But and if that servant say in his heart, My lord delayeth his coming; and shall begin to beat the menservants and maidens, and to eat and drink, and to be drunken; The lord of that servant will come in a day when he looketh not for *him*, and at an hour when he is not aware, and will cut him in sunder, and will appoint him his portion with the unbelievers. And that servant, which knew his lord's will, and prepared not *himself*, neither did according to his will, shall be beaten with many *stripes*. But he that knew not, and did commit things worthy of stripes, shall be beaten with few *stripes*. For unto whomsoever much is given, of him shall be much required: and to whom men have committed much, of him they will ask the more. I am come to send fire on the earth; and what will I, if it be already kindled? But I have a baptism to be baptized with; and how am I straitened till it be accomplished! *Suppose ye that I am come to give peace on earth? I tell you, Nay; but rather division: For from henceforth there shall be five* in one house divided, three against two, and two against three. The father shall be divided against the son, and the son against the father; the mother against the daughter, and the daughter against the mother; the mother in law against her daughter in law, and the daughter in law against her mother in law" (Luke 12:41–53 KJV, emphasis mine).

This parable is about Israel missing the first coming of Jesus and the results of that. Jesus then rebukes them for not discerning the time of visitation.

"And he said also to the people, When ye see a cloud rise out of the west, straightway ye say, There cometh a shower; and so it is. And when *ye see* the south wind blow, ye say, There will be heat; and it cometh to pass. *Ye hypocrites, ye can discern the face of the sky and of the earth; but how is it that ye do not discern this time?* Yea, and why even of yourselves judge ye not what is right?" (Luke 12:54–57 KJV, emphasis mine).

The day of visitation (Jesus's first coming) was perplexing for the Jews. It was shrouded in mystery for the purpose of Jesus's rejection and crucifixion, and the gospel then going to the Gentiles.

"For I would not, brethren, that ye should be ignorant of this *mystery,* lest ye should be wise in your own conceits; *that blindness in part is happened to Israel, until the fulness of the Gentiles be come in*" (Romans 11:25 KJV, emphasis mine).

If Israel had received Jesus as Messiah, the gospel would not have been given unto the Gentiles. This rejection was God's plan the whole time, and he prophesied this in many different ways.

Jesus said that he came to bring division. Jesus's first coming "visitation" created division among families. Many people accepted Jesus as Messiah and members of their own families turned against them. Many betrayed their own family members, handing them over to the authorities. Let's continue in Matthew 24.

"But he that shall endure unto the end, the same shall be saved. And this gospel of the kingdom shall be preached in all the world for a witness unto all nations; and then shall the end come" (Matt. 24:13–14 KJV, emphasis mine).

I have already mentioned what the end actually is. Instead of the end of the world as we know it, it is the end of the old covenant system, the end of Israel as a nation for a time, and the kingdom of God being removed from Israel and given over to the Gentiles. This is supported by the context of the Scripture in Matthew 24. Every other Scripture there is situated in the first century; it doesn't make sense for the Scripture to jump more than 2000 years in the future. Again, Jesus said it would come upon "that generation" to whom he was speaking. Let's look at the Scripture to confirm this.

"God, who at sundry times and in divers manners spake in time past unto the fathers by the prophets, *Hath in these last days* spoken unto us by *his* Son, whom he hath appointed heir of all things, by whom also he made the worlds" (Heb. 1:1–2 KJV, emphasis mine).

The writer of Hebrews calls the days when Jesus spoke to them the "last days."

"Forasmuch as ye know that ye were not redeemed with corruptible things, *as* silver and gold, from your vain conversation *received* by tradition from your fathers; But with the precious blood of Christ, as of a lamb without blemish and without spot: Who verily was foreordained before the foundation of the world, but was manifest in *these last times* for you" (1 Peter 1:18–20 KJV, emphasis mine).

Here, Peter calls the time in which Jesus was manifested the "last times."

"But Peter, standing up with the eleven, lifted up his voice, and said unto them, Ye men of Judaea, and all *ye* that dwell at Jerusalem, be this known unto you, and hearken to my words: For these are not drunken, as ye suppose, seeing it is *but* the third hour of the day. But this is that which was spoken by the prophet Joel; And it shall come to pass *in the last days*, saith God, I will pour out of my Spirit upon all flesh: and your sons and your daughters shall prophesy, and your young men shall see visions, and your old men shall dream dreams" (Acts 2:14–17 KJV, emphasis mine).

Peter again declares that on the day of Pentecost, the Spirit would be poured out in the "last days." Because this did occur, this shows that time period to be the "last days."

"Little children, it is the *last time*: and as ye have heard that antichrist shall come, even now are there many antichrists; whereby *we know that it is the last time*" (1 John 2:18 KJV, emphasis mine).

John says, "it is the last time." How did he know? It's very simple, he had seen antichrists or false Christs—the ones Jesus warned him about in Matthew 24. Remember, John was there, and he agrees with the others: the generation during his lifetime was the generation of the last days.

Right now, you may be thinking, but Scripture says the gospel had to be preached in ALL THE WORLD and then the end would come. That's a great point. Remember when Jesus was born? Why did Joseph and Mary have to go to Bethlehem? A tax was declared. Who had to pay that tax?

"And it came to pass in those days, that there went out a decree from Caesar Augustus, *that all the world should be taxed. (And* this taxing was first made when Cyrenius was governor of Syria.) And all went to be taxed, every one into his own city" (Luke 2:1–3 KJV, emphasis mine).

"All the world should be taxed." Did the Chinese pay these taxes? No. Why? They were not part of the Roman Empire. Here, the "world" refers to the whole Roman Empire, and there is a chance that "the whole world" in Matthew 24 means the whole Roman Empire. Does this fit? If the "end" is the end of Israel, Jerusalem, and the old covenant, and the gospel was preached in the Roman Empire before the end in 70 A.D., that would fit. However, speculation will get us nowhere; let's see if the Bible proves this out. Do you remember the vision that Daniel interpreted for King Nebuchadnezzar?

"The king answered and said to Daniel, whose name *was* Belteshazzar, Art thou able to make known unto me the dream which I have seen, and the interpretation thereof? Daniel answered in the presence of the king, and said, The secret which the king hath demanded cannot the wise *men*, the astrologers, the magicians, the soothsayers, shew unto the king; But there is a God in heaven that revealeth secrets, and maketh known to the king Nebuchadnezzar *what shall be in the latter days.* Thy dream, and the visions of thy head upon thy bed, are these" (Dan. 2:26–28 KJV, emphasis mine).

This vision was to be accomplished in the "latter days," which our study has pointed toward as the days of Jesus until 70 A.D. Daniel will interpret something that would come to pass in the days of Jesus or shortly thereafter.

"As for thee, O king, thy thoughts came *into thy mind* upon thy bed, what should come to pass hereafter: and he that revealeth secrets maketh known to thee what shall come to pass. But as for me, this secret is not revealed to me for *any* wisdom that I have more than any living, but for *their* sakes that shall make known the interpretation to the king, and that thou mightest know the thoughts of thy heart.

Thou, O king, sawest, and behold a great image. This great image, whose brightness *was* excellent, stood before thee; and the form thereof *was* terrible. This image's head *was* of fine gold, his breast and his arms of silver, his belly and his thighs of brass, His legs of iron, his feet part of iron and part of clay. Thou sawest till that a stone was cut out without hands, which smote the image upon his feet *that were* of iron and clay, and brake them to pieces. Then was the iron, the clay, the brass, the silver, and the gold, broken to pieces together, and became like the chaff of the summer threshingfloors; and the wind carried them away, that no place was found for them: and the stone that smote the image became a great mountain, and filled the whole earth. This *is* the dream; and we will tell the interpretation thereof before the king. Thou, O king, *art* a king of kings: for the God of heaven hath given thee a kingdom, power, and strength, and glory. And wheresoever the children of men dwell, the beasts of the field and the fowls of the heaven hath he given into thine hand, and hath made thee ruler over them all. Thou *art* this head of gold. And after thee shall arise another kingdom inferior to thee, and another third kingdom of brass, which shall bear rule over all the earth. And the fourth kingdom shall be strong as iron: forasmuch as iron breaketh in pieces and subdueth all *things*: and as iron that breaketh all these, shall it break in pieces and bruise. And whereas thou sawest the feet and toes, part of potters' clay, and part of iron, the kingdom shall be divided; but there shall be in it of the strength of the iron, forasmuch as thou sawest the iron mixed with miry clay. And *as* the toes of the feet *were* part of iron, and part of clay, so the kingdom shall be partly strong, and partly broken. And whereas thou sawest iron mixed with miry clay, they shall mingle themselves with the seed of men: but they shall not cleave one to another, even as iron is not mixed with clay. And in the days of these kings shall the God of heaven set up a kingdom, which shall never be destroyed: and the kingdom shall not be left to other people, *but* it shall break in pieces and consume all these kingdoms, and it shall stand for ever. Forasmuch as thou sawest that the stone was cut out of the mountain without hands, and that it brake in pieces the iron, the brass, the clay, the silver, and the gold; the great God hath made known to the king what shall come to pass hereafter: and the dream *is* certain, and the interpretation thereof sure" (Dan. 2:29–45 KJV).

This prophecy regards the four kingdoms that would come to power on the earth, marking the time that Messiah would appear. The four kingdoms were: the Babylonians, who ruled at the time of the vision; the Medo-Persians; the Greek Empire; and the Roman Empire. The purpose of this prophecy was to announce that one kingdom would be built that would never pass away. The Jews pointed to this prophecy as evidence that the Messiah would appear and build or restore the "kingdom" to Israel in the days of the fourth kingdom (the Roman Empire). The problem here was that the kingdom was a spiritual one, rather than the physical one they were expecting. Jesus taught many parables about the "kingdom of God" to show how the real kingdom would operate, and Jesus received that kingdom at the time of his resurrection.

"Being made so much better than the angels, as he hath by inheritance obtained a more excellent name than they. For unto which of the angels said he at any time, Thou art my Son, this day have I begotten thee? And again, I will be to him a Father, and he shall be to me a Son? And again, when he bringeth in the firstbegotten into the world, he saith, And let all the angels of God worship him. And of the angels he saith, Who maketh his angels spirits, and his ministers a flame of fire. *But unto the Son he saith, Thy throne, O God, is for ever and ever: a sceptre of righteousness is the sceptre of thy kingdom.* Thou hast loved righteousness, and hated iniquity; therefore God, *even* thy God, hath anointed thee with the oil of gladness above thy fellows. And, Thou, Lord, in the beginning hast laid the foundation of the earth; and the heavens are the works of thine hands: They shall perish; but thou remainest; and they all shall wax old as doth a garment; And as a vesture shalt thou fold them up, and they shall be changed: but thou art the same, and thy years shall not fail"(Heb. 1:4–12 KJV, emphasis mine).

We also receive that kingdom when we are born again.

"And this *word*, Yet once more, signifieth the removing of those things that are shaken, as of things that are made, that those things which cannot be shaken may remain. *Wherefore we receiving a kingdom which cannot be moved*, let us have grace, whereby we may serve God acceptably with reverence and godly fear: For our God *is* a consuming fire" (Heb. 12:27–29 KJV, emphasis mine).

Since the "kingdom" was created during the Roman Empire, what did the Scripture say would happen?

"And in the days of these kings shall the God of heaven set up a kingdom, which shall never be destroyed: and the kingdom shall not be left to other people, *but* it shall break in pieces *and consume all these kingdoms*, and it shall stand for ever" (Dan. 2:43–44 KJV, emphasis mine).

When the "kingdom of God" came into existence, it would devour the other kingdoms. The Roman Empire controlled all the lands that the other three kingdoms had once conquered. This means the gospel had to be preached throughout all of the world, which was the Roman Empire. The gospel or the "kingdom" would consume that empire when it was shared throughout the world and the end came. The Apostle Paul preached to Roman authorities during his trial. Rome was the center of the world at this time, and the good news of Jesus, once preached in Rome, spread throughout the empire and eventually consumed the whole kingdom.

Now you can see how the gospel was preached in all the world and the end came during the first century. It's quite amazing. Let's continue our study.

"When ye therefore shall see the abomination of desolation, spoken of by Daniel the prophet, stand in the holy place, (whoso readeth, let him understand:) Then let them which be in Judaea flee into the mountains: Let him which is on the housetop not come down to take any thing out of his house: Neither let him which is in the field return back to take his clothes. And woe unto them that are with child, and to them that give suck in those days! But pray ye that your flight be not in the winter, neither on the sabbath day: For then shall be great tribulation, such as was not since the beginning of the world to this time, no, nor ever shall be" (Matt. 24:15–21 KJV).

If you have studied end time prophecy, you must have wondered about the abomination of desolation. There are many theories out there, but theories don't take us anywhere. Like you, I am committed to finding the truth.

In our study, we have seen how Matthew 24 was fulfilled in the first century. Let's see if we can establish the timing of the abomination of desolation in the first century, as well.

Let me point out that in verse 19, Jesus warns those who have children during the time of the abomination of desolation. He tells them to pray that their escape would not be in the winter, because of the cold, nor on the Sabbath, because they could only travel a certain distance on the Sabbath, in keeping with Jewish law. This sounds very similar to a warning Jesus gave to the women of Jerusalem on his way to the cross.

"And as they led him away, they laid hold upon one Simon, a Cyrenian, coming out of the country, and on him they laid the cross, that he might bear *it* after Jesus. And there followed him a great company of people, and of women, which also bewailed and lamented him. But Jesus turning unto them said, *Daughters of Jerusalem, weep not for me, but weep for yourselves, and for your children. For, behold, the days are coming, in the which they shall say, Blessed are the barren, and the wombs that never bare, and the paps which never gave suck.* Then shall they begin to say to the mountains, Fall on us; and to the hills, Cover us. For if they do these things in a green tree, what shall be done in the dry?" (Luke 23:26–31 KJV, emphasis mine).

Jesus warns the Daughters of Jerusalem that they and their children would see the days in which they would say, "Blessed are the barren." In other words, something terrible would occur during the generation to whom Jesus was speaking. Could these two Scriptures be talking about the same event? Let's compare Scriptures to see if this is possible. Because Luke also wrote about this subject, we will first read Matthew and then Luke.

"And then shall many be offended, and shall betray one another, and shall hate one another. And many false prophets shall rise, and shall deceive many. And because iniquity shall abound, the love of many shall wax cold. But he that shall endure unto the end, the same shall be saved. And this gospel of the kingdom shall be preached in all the world for a witness unto all nations; and then shall the end come. *When ye therefore shall see the abomination of desolation, spoken of by Daniel the prophet, stand in the holy place, (whoso readeth, let him understand:) Then let them which be in Judaea flee into the mountains: Let him which is on the housetop not come down to take any thing out of his house: Neither let him which is in the field return back to take his clothes. And woe unto them that are with child, and to them that give suck in those days! But pray ye that your flight be not in the winter, neither on the sabbath day: For then shall be great tribulation, such as was not since the beginning of the world to this time, no, nor ever shall be"* (Matt. 24:9–21 KJV, emphasis mine).

"And ye shall be betrayed both by parents, and brethren, and kinsfolks, and friends; and *some* of you shall they cause to be put to death. And ye shall be hated of all *men* for my name's sake. But there shall not an hair of your head perish. In your patience possess ye your souls.

And when ye shall see Jerusalem compassed with armies, then know that the desolation thereof is nigh. Then let them which are in Judaea flee to the mountains; and let them which are in the midst of it depart out; and let not them that are in the countries enter thereinto. *For these be the days of vengeance, that all things which are written may be fulfilled. But woe unto them that are with child, and to them that give suck, in those days! for there shall be great distress in the land, and wrath upon this people.* And they shall fall by the edge of the sword, and shall be led away captive into all nations: and Jerusalem shall be trodden down of the Gentiles, until the times of the Gentiles be fulfilled" (Luke 21:16–24 KJV, emphasis mine).

Did you see the difference? Instead of saying the "abomination of desolation," this warns that when Jerusalem is surrounded with armies, its time of desolation or destruction is near. Jesus is telling them to flee when the Roman armies surround Jerusalem, or the armies will kill or capture them! And, that is exactly what happened in 70 A.D.

It makes sense that the abomination of desolation is the destruction of Jerusalem and the temple in 70 A.D. These were the days of vengeance. What was the vengeance for? Many times when God sent a prophet, Israel rejected them and killed him. God did not bring a full judgment to bear upon the people for that because their sins were forgiven through the spilled blood of animal sacrifices, but when Israel rejected Jesus, they rejected their own path to forgiveness. After Jesus, their sins could no longer be forgiven through animal sacrifice because the only way to God was through Jesus. Since Israel did not accept Jesus, God had to judge or take vengeance upon the Jewish people for their sins. Here is what Jesus said:

"Wherefore, behold, I send unto you prophets, and wise men, and scribes: and *some* of them ye shall kill and crucify; and *some* of them shall ye scourge in your synagogues, and persecute *them* from city to city: *That upon you may come all the righteous blood shed upon the earth, from the blood of righteous Abel unto the blood of Zacharias son of Barachias, whom ye slew between the temple and the altar. Verily I say unto you, All these things shall come upon this generation*" (Matt. 23:34–36 KJV, emphasis mine).

The abomination of desolation is the vengeance of God upon Israel for rejecting Jesus.

This Scripture also says that there would be great tribulation in those days. Well, I suppose so! Jerusalem would be ransacked by the Romans, so of course there would be tribulation. This is also the Scripture that prophecy teachers use to talk about "the great tribulation," which they teach as a seven-year period during which the Antichrist takes over the whole world sometime in the future. I have already proved this theory false, but I wanted to mention the next part of that same verse.

"For then shall be great tribulation, such as was not since the beginning of the world to this time, *no, nor ever shall be*" (Matt. 24:20–21 KJV, emphasis mine).

This says that that particular tribulation had never happened before, nor would it ever happen again. This means there is no chance that a parallel of this tribulation might happen again in the future.

Let's get back to Mathew.

"And except those days should be shortened, there should no flesh be saved: but for the elect's sake those days shall be shortened" (Matt. 24:22 KJV).

This Scripture is simply saying that if this tribulation was not shortened, all of Israel would be killed. The elect (believers in Jesus) were the reason why God shortened the tribulation. He saved a remnant out of Israel. There are many types and shadows concerning a remnant, and they all are pointing to this time in history. Remember the time of Elijah, when Israel was in rebellion and serving Baal as their God. Elijah grew tired of running and cried out to God, saying, I'm the last one serving you. God said, I have reserved 7000 (a remnant) unto myself. See 1 Kings 19:1–18. You can look up "remnant" and see all of the parallels between the time of the prophecy and the time of Jesus. The Apostle Paul confirms that this came to pass.

"I say then, Hath God cast away his people? God forbid. For I also am an Israelite, of the seed of Abraham, *of* the tribe of Benjamin. God hath not cast away his people which he foreknew. Wot ye not what the Scripture saith of Elias? how he maketh intercession to God against Israel, saying, Lord, they have killed thy prophets, and digged down thine altars; and I am left alone, and they seek my life. But what saith the answer of God unto him? I have reserved to myself seven thousand men, who have not bowed the knee to *the image of* Baal. *Even so then at this present time also there is a remnant according to the election of grace*" (Romans 11:1–5 KJV, emphasis mine).

Isaiah prophesied against Israel in their rebellion before the Babylonian invasion. We previously discussed how the Babylonian invasion was a type and shadow of what would happen in the Roman era. God used the Babylonians to judge Israel in that time and then used the Romans to judge them later. Isaiah's prophesy applied in both instances. Here is one of those prophecies.

"The vision of Isaiah the son of Amoz, which he saw concerning Judah and Jerusalem in the days of Uzziah, Jotham, Ahaz, *and* Hezekiah, kings of Judah.

Hear, O heavens, and give ear, O earth: for the LORD hath spoken, I have nourished and brought up children, and they have rebelled against me. The ox knoweth his owner, and the ass his master's crib: *but* Israel doth not know, my people doth not consider. Ah sinful nation, a people laden with iniquity, a seed of evildoers, children that are corrupters: they have forsaken the LORD, they have provoked the Holy One of Israel unto anger, they are gone away backward. Why should ye be stricken any more? ye will revolt more and more: the whole head is sick, and the whole heart faint. From the sole of the foot even unto the head *there is* no soundness in it; *but* wounds, and bruises, and putrifying sores: they have not been closed, neither bound up, neither mollified with ointment. Your country *is* desolate, your cities *are* burned with fire: your land, strangers devour it in your presence, and *it is* desolate, as overthrown by strangers. And the daughter of Zion is left as a cottage in a vineyard, as a lodge in a garden of cucumbers, as a besieged city. *Except the LORD of hosts had left unto us a very small remnant, we should have been as Sodom, and we should have been like unto Gomorrah*" (Isaiah 1:1–9 KJV, emphasis mine).

God declares desolation upon the country, fire upon the city, and strangers devouring it in the presence of Israel. This sounds just like the abomination of desolation. Then, the Lord says essentially the same thing in Matthew 24. If God had not shortened that time period or left a very small remnant, Israel would have been destroyed, just like Sodom and Gomorrah. Let's continue.

"Then if any man shall say unto you, Lo, here *is* Christ, or there; believe *it* not. For there shall arise false Christs, and false prophets, and shall shew great signs and wonders; insomuch that, if *it were* possible, they shall deceive the very elect. Behold, I have told you before. Wherefore if they shall say unto you, Behold, he is in the desert; go not forth: behold, *he is* in the secret chambers; believe *it* not" (Matt. 24:23–26 KJV, emphasis mine).

Here again Jesus warns of false Christs and false prophets. Jesus foretells that these false prophets and messiahs would show great signs and wonders that could deceive the elect (believers in Jesus). Jesus also mentions two specific places where he would not appear. Remember that the Jews are still looking for a Messiah to fight the Romans, so they would look for the Messiah in the desert or in the secret chambers. At this point, the disciples still believe that Jesus will overthrow the Romans. They don't understand the truth. Jesus tells them not to go where the Jews say the Messiah is because that is where the trouble would be. The false messiahs would always start a rebellion against the Romans, and the constant rebellions would lead the Romans to destroy Jerusalem.

"For as the lightning cometh out of the east, and shineth even unto the west; so shall also the coming of the Son of man be. For wheresoever the carcass is, there will the eagles be gathered together. Immediately after the tribulation of those days shall the sun be darkened, and the moon shall not give her light, and the stars shall fall from heaven, and the powers of the heavens shall be shaken: And then shall appear the sign of the Son of man in heaven: and then shall all the tribes of the earth mourn, and they shall see the Son of man coming in the clouds of heaven with power and great glory" (Matt. 24:27–30 KJV).

"Immediately after the tribulation of those days" confirms the time period again. The tribulation is referring to the fall of Jerusalem. Did the sun, moon, and stars literally go out? They possibly did for a short time, but I have no way of confirming that. Using history and other means to interpret or confirm Scripture can be dangerous. History is written by those who win the wars, meaning that they have a biased point of view, which may not be the same as that of God. It's best to use major events in history on which many sources can agree, rather than focusing on little details that may not be accurately represented. For instance, it has been said that the false messiahs of the first century could produce signs and wonders and the Bible says the same, but knowing exactly what those were and building a belief upon them alone is dangerous. This is why I stick to general information that can be confirmed. All of the history I have discussed in this book can be easily found with a little research. If you are a serious Bible student, you will research and study all of these things for yourself. Don't put your trust in me or in anyone else. God is the only one who should be trusted. I can't stress enough the importance of confirming Scripture with Scripture; that is the only way to know the answers for sure.

Anyway, I will step off my soapbox now and return to our study. The description of the sun and moon withdrawing their light and the stars falling from the sky has been used in the Old Testament before to indicate judgment upon someone. For instance:

"The burden of Babylon, which Isaiah the son of Amoz did see. Lift ye up a banner upon the high mountain, exalt the voice unto them, shake the hand, that they may go into the gates of the nobles. I have commanded my sanctified ones, I have also called my mighty ones for mine anger, *even* them that rejoice in my highness. The noise of a multitude in the mountains, like as of a great people; a tumultuous noise of the kingdoms of nations gathered together: the LORD of hosts mustereth the host of the battle. They come from a far country, from the end of heaven, *even* the LORD, and the weapons of his indignation, to destroy the whole land.

Howl ye; for the day of the LORD *is* at hand; it shall come as a destruction from the Almighty. Therefore shall all hands be faint, and every man's heart shall melt: And they shall be afraid: pangs and sorrows shall take hold of them; they shall be in pain as a woman that travaileth: they shall be amazed one at another; their faces *shall be as* flames. Behold, the day of the LORD cometh, cruel both with wrath and fierce anger, to lay the land desolate: and he shall destroy the sinners thereof out of it. *For the stars of heaven and the constellations thereof shall not give their light: the sun shall be darkened in his going forth, and the moon shall not cause her light to shine.* And I will punish the world for *their* evil, and the wicked for their iniquity; and I will cause the arrogancy of the proud to cease, and will lay low the haughtiness of the terrible. I will make a man more precious than fine gold; even a man than the golden wedge of Ophir. Therefore I will shake the heavens, and the earth shall remove out of her place, in the wrath of the LORD of hosts, and in the day of his fierce anger. And it shall be as the chased roe, and as a sheep that no man taketh up: they shall every man turn to his own people, and flee every one into his own land. Every one that is found shall be thrust through; and every one that is joined *unto them* shall fall by the sword. Their children also shall be dashed to pieces before their eyes; their houses shall be spoiled, and their wives ravished. Behold, I will stir up the Medes against them, which shall not regard silver; and *as for* gold, they shall not delight in it. *Their* bows also shall dash the young men to pieces; and they shall have no pity on the fruit of the womb; their eye shall not spare children.

And Babylon, the glory of kingdoms, the beauty of the Chaldees' excellency, shall be as when God overthrew Sodom and Gomorrah. It shall never be inhabited, neither shall it be dwelt in from generation to generation: neither shall the Arabian pitch tent there; neither shall the shepherds make their fold there. But wild beasts of the desert shall lie there; and their houses shall be full of doleful creatures; and owls shall dwell there, and satyrs shall dance there. And the wild beasts of the islands shall cry in their desolate houses, and dragons in *their* pleasant palaces: and her time *is* near to come, and her days shall not be prolonged" (Isaiah 13:1–22 KJV, emphasis mine).

This is a prophecy concerning the judgment or destruction of Babylon by the Medes, which was the second empire to rule in Daniel's prophecy. Did you notice how God uses the sun, moon, and stars to speak of judgment? This is judgment language. Let's look at another example.

"And it came to pass in the twelfth year, in the twelfth month, in the first *day* of the month, *that* the word of the LORD came unto me, saying, Son of man, take up a lamentation for Pharaoh king of Egypt, and say unto him, Thou art like a young lion of the nations, and thou *art* as a whale in the seas: and thou camest forth with thy rivers, and troubledst the waters with thy feet, and fouledst their rivers. Thus saith the Lord GOD; I will therefore spread out my net over thee with a company of many people; and they shall bring thee up in my net. Then will I leave thee upon the land, I will cast thee forth upon the open field, and will cause all the fowls of the heaven to remain upon thee, and I will fill the beasts of the whole earth with thee. And I will lay thy flesh upon the mountains, and fill the valleys with thy height. I will also water with thy blood the land wherein thou swimmest, *even* to the mountains; and the rivers shall be full of thee. *And when I shall put thee out, I will cover the heaven, and make the stars thereof dark; I will cover the sun with a cloud, and the moon shall not give her light. All the bright lights of heaven will I make dark over thee, and set darkness upon thy land,* saith the Lord GOD. I will also vex the hearts of many people, when I shall bring thy destruction among the nations, into the countries which thou hast not known. Yea, I will make many people amazed at thee, and their kings shall be horribly afraid for thee, when I shall brandish my sword before them; and they shall tremble at *every* moment, every man for his own life, in the day of thy fall. For thus saith the Lord GOD; The sword of the king of Babylon shall come upon thee. By the swords of the mighty will I cause thy multitude to fall, the terrible of the nations, all of them: and they shall spoil the pomp of Egypt, and all the multitude thereof shall be destroyed. I will destroy also all the beasts thereof from beside the great waters; neither shall the foot of man trouble them any more, nor the hoofs of beasts trouble them. Then will I make their waters deep, and cause their rivers to run like oil, saith the Lord GOD. When I shall make the land of Egypt desolate, and the country shall be destitute of that whereof it was full, when I shall smite all them that dwell therein, then shall they know that I *am* the LORD. This *is* the lamentation wherewith they shall lament her: the daughters of the nations shall lament her: they shall lament for her, *even* for Egypt, and for all her multitude, saith the Lord GOD" (Ezek. 32:1–16 KJV, emphasis mine).

Again, it's possible that this could have been literal, but it is definitely speaking of an imminent judgment upon Egypt. We can take this to mean the same as in our study in Matthew. This is also an indication of an imminent judgment upon someone, namely Israel.

Now let's turn to the "Son of Man coming in the clouds of Heaven with power and great glory." What does this mean? Is this talking about Jesus's second coming? It can't possibly be the second coming of Christ because just a few verses later, it states:

"Verily I say unto you, This generation shall not pass, till all these things be fulfilled" (Matt. 24:34 KJV).

Everything mentioned before this had to happen in the generation to whom Jesus was speaking.

Jesus used that statement in another setting as well. Do you remember when he came before the high priest at his trial? The high priest asked Jesus if he was the Christ. Here is that passage.

"We heard him say, I will destroy this temple that is made with hands, and within three days I will build another made without hands. But neither so did their witness agree together. And the high priest stood up in the midst, and asked Jesus, saying, Answerest thou nothing? what *is it which* these witness against thee? But he held his peace, and answered nothing. Again the high priest asked him, and said unto him, Art thou the Christ, the Son of the Blessed? And Jesus said, *I am: and ye shall see the Son of man sitting on the right hand of power, and coming in the clouds of heaven.* Then the high priest rent his clothes, and saith, What need we any further witnesses? Ye have heard the blasphemy: what think ye? And they all condemned him to be guilty of death" (Mark 14:58–64 KJV, emphasis mine).

The high priest asked if Jesus is the Christ. Jesus says, yes and YOU shall see the Son of man sitting on the right hand of power, and coming in the clouds of heaven. Jesus said that the high priest would be able to see Jesus coming in the clouds of heaven. Puzzling, isn't it? We have to understand that Jesus's statement was offensive to the high priest for two reasons. First, Jesus claimed to be the Messiah, and the high priest rejected that wholeheartedly. Second, Jesus quoted a Messianic Scripture to him as well, again saying he is the one.

The problem was that the high priest and others believed in a different interpretation of the Scripture that Jesus quoted.

"I saw in the night visions, and, behold, *one like the Son of man came with the clouds of heaven,* and came to the Ancient of days, and they brought him near before him. *And there was given him dominion, and glory, and a kingdom,* that all people, nations, and languages, should serve him: his dominion *is* an everlasting dominion, which shall not pass away, *and his kingdom that which shall not be destroyed*" (Dan. 7:13–14 KJV, emphasis mine).

The interpretation of that day was literal. What I mean is, the Son of Man (Messiah) would literally come with the clouds of heaven and be given dominion and glory, with a PHYSICAL kingdom. All of Israel believed that a physical kingdom would be restored to them, and they missed the spiritual kingdom. We know that the Son of Man is Jesus, but when was Jesus brought near before the Ancient of Days (Father God)? Jesus was presented to Father God as the spotless Lamb that took away the sin of the world after his resurrection. That is when he received the kingdom that shall not be destroyed. We also receive the kingdom that cannot be moved when we are born again. The writer of Hebrews states it this way.

"And this word, Yet once more, signifieth the removing of those things that are shaken, as of things that are made, that those things which cannot be shaken may remain. Wherefore *we receiving a kingdom which cannot be moved,* let us have grace, whereby we may serve God acceptably with reverence and godly fear" (Heb. 12:27–28 KJV, emphasis mine).

The point I am trying to make here is that the Scripture Jesus quoted to the High Priest was fulfilled at his first coming, not the second coming of Christ. The sign of the Son of Man coming in the clouds of Heaven was the fact that the Romans overcame Israel and their false Messiah. This was the sign showing them that their interpretation of Scripture was sorely incorrect. They began to mourn because they missed it! In fact, read how Jesus said it to the Pharisees.

"And when he was demanded of the Pharisees, when the kingdom of God should come, he answered them and said, The kingdom of God cometh not with observation: Neither shall they say, Lo here! or, lo there! for, behold, the kingdom of God is within you" (Luke 17:20–21 KJV).

The Pharisees demand that Jesus tell them when he will bring the kingdom (and rise up against the Romans). Jesus tells them, you will not physically see the kingdom of God because it is inside you. He says, you will want to see this physical kingdom. Look at where Jesus takes the conversation after that.

"And he said unto the disciples, The days will come, when ye shall desire to see one of the days of the Son of man, and ye shall not see *it*. And they shall say to you, See here; or, see there: go not after *them*, nor follow *them*. For as the lightning, that lighteneth out of the one *part* under heaven, shineth unto the other *part* under heaven; so shall also the Son of man be in his day. But first must he suffer many things, and be rejected of this generation. And as it was in the days of Noe, so shall it be also in the days of the Son of man. They did eat, they drank, they married wives, they were given in marriage, until the day that Noe entered into the ark, and the flood came, and destroyed them all. Likewise also as it was in the days of Lot; they did eat, they drank, they bought, they sold, they planted, they builded; But the same day that Lot went out of Sodom it rained fire and brimstone from heaven, and destroyed *them* all. *Even thus shall it be in the day when the Son of man is revealed*. In that day, he which shall be upon the housetop, and his stuff in the house, let him not come down to take it away: and he that is in the field, let him likewise not return back. Remember Lot's wife. Whosoever shall seek to save his life shall lose it; and whosoever shall lose his life shall preserve it. I tell you, in that night there shall be two *men* in one bed; the one shall be taken, and the other shall be left. Two *women* shall be grinding together; the one shall be taken, and the other left. Two *men* shall be in the field; the one shall be taken, and the other left. And they answered and said unto him, Where, Lord? And he said unto them, Wheresoever the body *is*, thither will the eagles be gathered together" (Luke 17:21–37 KJV, emphasis mine).

Does that sound familiar? It sounds just like Matthew 24, doesn't it? Let's move back to Matthew.

"And he shall send his angels with a great sound of a trumpet, and they shall gather together his elect from the four winds, from one end of heaven to the other" (Matt. 24:31 KJV).

I wish I could tell you more about this Scripture, but God has not yet revealed to me exactly what this means. I don't want to speculate on my ideas of what it means. I can't confirm them yet, so I will keep them to myself until God gives me more insight.

"Now learn a parable of the fig tree; When his branch is yet tender, and putteth forth leaves, ye know that summer *is* nigh: So likewise ye, when ye shall see *all* these things, know that it is near, *even* at the doors. *Verily I say unto you, This generation shall not pass, till all these things be fulfilled.* Heaven and earth shall pass away, but my words shall not pass away" (Matt. 24:32–35 KJV, emphasis mine).

Jesus emphatically says all these things will happen in "this generation." So, it is not right for us to take anything from this and try to make it a future fulfillment in our time. That just doesn't work. Jesus wants us to understand the parable of the fig tree. When the branch is tender and puts forth leaves, know that summer is near. When they saw the things Jesus said would come to pass, they should have known that the end was near. This reminds me of something. I notice that Jesus does not say anything about the figs on the tree. It reminds me of when Jesus cursed the fig tree.

"And on the morrow, when they were come from Bethany, he was hungry: And seeing a fig tree afar off having leaves, he came, if haply he might find any thing thereon: and when he came to it, *he found nothing but leaves*; for the time of figs was not *yet*. And Jesus answered and said unto it, No man eat fruit of thee hereafter for ever" (Mark 11:12–14 KJV, emphasis mine).

Isn't it interesting that Jesus found only leaves on this fig tree, when he desired fruit from that tree? It wasn't time for the figs to grow on the tree, and Jesus then cursed that fig tree.

"And they come to Jerusalem: and Jesus went into the temple, and began to cast out them that sold and bought in the temple, and overthrew the tables of the moneychangers, and the seats of them that sold doves; And would not suffer that any man should carry *any* vessel through the temple. And he taught, saying unto them, Is it not written, My house shall be called of all nations the house of prayer? but ye have made it a den of thieves. And the scribes and chief priests heard *it*, and sought how they might destroy him: for they feared him, because all the people was astonished at his doctrine. And when even was come, he went out of the city. And in the morning, as they passed by, they saw the fig tree dried up from the roots. And Peter calling to remembrance saith unto him, Master, behold, the fig tree which thou cursedst is withered away" (Mark 11:14–21 KJV).

The fig tree withered away from its roots. This is prophetic of Israel. Israel is cursed because they rejected their own forgiveness (Jesus). The animal sacrifices no longer removed their sins, and therefore the curse of the law (see Deut. 28) came upon them.

"But of that day and hour knoweth no *man*, no, not the angels of heaven, but my Father only. But as the days of Noe *were*, so shall also the coming of the Son of man be. For as in the days that were before the flood they were eating and drinking, marrying and giving in marriage, until the day that Noe entered into the ark, And knew not until the flood came, and took them all away; so shall also the coming of the Son of man be" (Matt. 24:36–39 KJV).

What day is Jesus talking about? It's the day of vengeance, the day of the wrath of the Lamb. Israel did not know or understand that God was going to judge them. The coming of the Son of Man is the coming in judgment upon Israel, which would take them by surprise. They simply continued with their daily lives until the Romans decided to destroy their way of life and scatter them across the world. Just as in the days of Noah, the people didn't believe and enter the ark (Jesus), and therefore, they were caught unaware and destroyed because of their lack of faith. Do you remember Jesus asking when the Son of Man comes, will he find faith on the earth?

"And he spake a parable unto them *to this end*, that men ought always to pray, and not to faint; Saying, There was in a city a judge, which feared not God, neither regarded man: And there was a widow in that city; and she came unto him, saying, Avenge me of mine adversary. And he would not for a while: but afterward he said within himself, Though I fear not God, nor regard man; Yet because this widow troubleth me, I will avenge her, lest by her continual coming she weary me. And the Lord said, Hear what the unjust judge saith. And shall not God avenge his own elect, which cry day and night unto him, though he bear long with them? I tell you that he will avenge them speedily. Nevertheless when the Son of man cometh, shall he find faith on the earth?" (Luke 18:1–8 KJV).

I wondered for a long time about this parable. I simply didn't understand what Jesus was talking about. It's really simple, though, when you receive a revelation from the Lord. The parable mentions God avenging his elect. Where have we heard that before? We learned in Chapter 5 of Luke that God would avenge the blood of the prophets because their blood cries out unto him for judgment. Jesus said God would avenge them speedily, and then asks if the Son of Man will find faith when he comes. When he comes to do what? Will he find faith when he pours out the wrath of the Lamb, "the day of vengeance of our God" (see Isaiah 61:2)? Jesus did not find faith when he came in judgment upon Israel, because if there had been faith, there would have been no need for judgment. This parable is referring to the time of vengeance in 70 A.D. No one expected this to happen except Jesus.

"Then shall two be in the field; the one shall be taken, and the other left. Two *women shall be* grinding at the mill; the one shall be taken, and the other left. Watch therefore: for ye know not what hour your Lord doth come. But know this, that if the goodman of the house had known in what watch the thief would come, he would have watched, and would not have suffered his house to be broken up. Therefore be ye also ready: for in such an hour as ye think not the Son of man cometh" (Matt. 24:40–44 KJV).

This shows that when the Son of Man comes, two will be in the field, one taken and the other left. The Romans came and separated families, scattering them all over the Roman Empire. Many were killed or forced into slavery. Jesus warns them to watch because they will not know when the Lord will come (in judgment). Jesus tells them that they can be saved from the judgment if they stay ready and watch for the signs. When they see the signs of the judgment, they must leave.

"Who then is a faithful and wise servant, whom his lord hath made ruler over his household, to give them meat in due season? Blessed *is* that servant, whom his lord when he cometh shall find so doing. Verily I say unto you, That he shall make him ruler over all his goods. But and if that evil servant shall say in his heart, My lord delayeth his coming; And shall begin to smite *his* fellowservants, and to eat and drink with the drunken; The lord of that servant shall come in a day when he looketh not for *him*, and in an hour that he is not aware of, And shall cut him asunder, and appoint *him* his portion with the hypocrites: there shall be weeping and gnashing of teeth" (Matt. 24:45–51 KJV).

The evil servant believes that the Lord delayed his coming. Why? Remember that the Jewish people were still looking for the Messiah after Jesus. No one had appeared who fit their expectations, so eventually they became very frustrated, and many gave up on the coming of the Messiah. And, that's when Jesus came in judgment.

We have now discussed the entire chapter of Matthew 24. When the context is revealed, you can see what the Scripture is speaking of. Study these things for yourself and see if they are true. Don't just take my word for it. Do your homework and find out the truth for yourself. I could have made a mistake and missed some things. I thank God that I am still learning, too.

Throughout this book, it has been my intention to show how to interpret Scripture properly. God has made a way for us to interpret Scripture and confirm that our interpretation is correct. I pray that you will not only use these principles to interpret end time events, but also for all of the doctrines of your beliefs. Make sure that what you believe is the truth. If this is done, we can remove many of the divisions in the body of Christ concerning doctrine. This is the reason why we have so many different denominations in the first place. People assert their own ideas of the truth, rather than relying on God's version, even though through study we can know and understand the truth of God's Word. I pray that the body of Christ will wake up and be "no longer tossed to and fro by every wind of doctrine." We have a job to do here on this earth! The salvation of many people in the world depends on us! It's time for the body of Christ to grow up and be like Jesus.

When the truth is discovered from the Bible, it changes the way we think. The truth of the revelation brought out in this book changes the way we see the end times. We now can understand that there will not be seven years of tribulation. If you have studied the end times, you have already seen why. Let me explain to those who have not studied it as much and may not have seen it yet. The seven years of tribulation come from Daniel 9:24–27. In Chapter 4 of this book, we discovered that the prophecy of the seventy weeks in Daniel 9:24–27 has already been fulfilled. The 490-year period has completely come to pass, which means there cannot be a 7-year period yet to be fulfilled in our future. Most prophecy teachers believe that only 483 years of that prophecy have passed, and there is a gap in fulfillment, meaning that 7 years are left to be fulfilled. This cannot be true if this prophecy was completely fulfilled the day Jesus was crucified. If you are still confused about this, read Chapter 4 again. Compare what is written here in this book with what Tim Lahaye, Jack Van Impe, Hal Lindsey, and others have written and taught on the subject.

If there are no 7 years of tribulation yet to be fulfilled, there is no Antichrist figure who will appear and rule the world for 7 years, either. To me, this doctrine doesn't make sense. Why would God "make an open show of Satan" to his shame (Col. 2:15) and then give the whole world to the Antichrist to destroy for seven years? Jesus took the keys of Death, Hell, and the Grave. Why would he then give that authority back to the Devil? The Devil has already been defeated completely! We are still here because we have to tell people about the Lord and enforce Satan's defeat.

If there is no Antichrist who will rule the world for 7 years, then the "signs of the times" that are preached today do not apply to us. People are looking for life on earth to grow worse and worse, when they ought to be enforcing the Devil's defeat. If the whole world is supposed to continually worsen, then Satan is not defeated. When the body of Christ realizes that Satan is under their feet, there will be a dominion exercised over him that has never been seen before. This doctrine of an Antichrist taking over the world actually makes Christians timid and fearful about the future. How many times have you heard someone say, "You know it must be the end of time—look at all the terrible things that are happening"? God is looking for a triumphant church, not a weak, fearful, and powerless one.

If there is no 7-year tribulation or Antichrist figure, then all the talk of a "revived Roman Empire" cannot be true either. All of those ideas are speculation, not interpretation.

The revelation in this book changes our perspective on our future, and it also changes the way we see many of Jesus's teachings. Now you can understand why Jesus taught about the kingdom of God so often. John said, Repent, for the kingdom of God is at hand. However, Israel did not understand the kingdom of God, so what did they think when they heard this? They thought of a physical kingdom that would rule the world because that is what they were expecting. And, that's why all of the parables of Jesus were so confusing to the Jews and to the disciples, for that matter. Jesus kept teaching them what the kingdom of God was really like, but they couldn't see it. Since the parables were about the kingdom of God, study them and see how many of them applied to Israel during Jesus's time. As far as I can see, every single one applies to them. There are some parables that teach principles that can be applied to us, but for the most part they are about Israel.

Some of you are probably thinking what I was thinking when God first revealed all these things to me. If all these things are either false or they have come to pass, what does our prophetic future really look like? What about the rapture of the church? Has that passed, too? Those are great questions. I will answer them in the following chapters as best as I can. There is still much to be discovered.

Chapter 9

9

WHAT HAPPENS AT THE RAPTURE?

THE RAPTURE OF THE CHURCH has been a hotly debated topic for a long time. One would claim the rapture would occur before the tribulation, another would say in the middle, and still another at the end of the tribulation. The question is, where does the rapture of the church fit when the tribulation spoken of in Daniel has already come and gone? With the fulfillment of the seventy weeks of Daniel, there cannot be a seven-year great tribulation.

Actually, what I am about to share with you is the first thing God revealed to me about the end times nearly ten years ago. This revelation is what started me looking in depth at the end times. After God showed this to me, I knew there was more to learn.

First, we must understand what the rapture is.

"Moreover, brethren, I declare unto you the gospel which I preached unto you, which also ye have received, and wherein ye stand; By which also ye are saved, if ye keep in memory what I preached unto you, unless ye have believed in vain. For I delivered unto you first of all that which I also received, how that Christ died for our sins according to the Scriptures; And that he was buried, and that he rose again the third day according to the Scriptures: And that he was seen of Cephas, then of the twelve: After that, he was seen of above five hundred brethren at once; of whom the greater part remain unto this present, but some are fallen asleep. After that, he was seen of James; then of all the apostles. And last of all he was seen of me also, as of one born out of due time. For I am the least of the apostles, that am not meet to be called an apostle, because I persecuted the church of God. But by the grace of God I am what I am: and his grace which *was bestowed* upon me was not in vain; but I laboured more abundantly than they all: yet not I, but the grace of God which was with me. Therefore whether *it were* I or they, so we preach, and so ye believed.

Now if Christ be preached that he rose from the dead, how say some among you that there is no resurrection of the dead?" (1 Cor. 15:1–12 KJV).

Paul begins to talk about how he preached that Jesus died for our sins, was buried, and on the third day rose bodily from the grave. There were some among the Corinthians who did not believe in a literal bodily resurrection from the dead. Paul begins to lay out his case for a bodily resurrection from the dead.

"But if there be no resurrection of the dead, then is Christ not risen: And if Christ be not risen, then *is* our preaching vain, and your faith *is* also vain. Yea, and we are found false witnesses of God; because we have testified of God that he raised up Christ: whom he raised not up, if so be that the dead rise not. For if the dead rise not, then is not Christ raised: And if Christ be not raised, your faith *is* vain; ye are yet in your sins. Then they also which are fallen asleep in Christ are perished. If in this life only we have hope in Christ, we are of all men most miserable" (1 Cor. 15:13–19 KJV).

Paul begins to list reasons why the resurrection is important:

1. If there is no resurrection of the dead, then Christ is not risen.
2. If Christ is not risen, preaching is in vain, and your faith is in vain.
3. Paul would be a false witness of God.
4. None of our sins would be forgiven.
5. All who have died are perished.
6. If we had hope only in this life, we are of all men most miserable.

What great logic Paul used! This resurrection is an important part of the gospel. Paul's logic says, if Christ rose from the dead and we are in Christ, we must also at some point be raised from the dead likewise. Paul then begins to share biblical insight.

"But now is Christ risen from the dead, *and* become the firstfruits of them that slept. For since by man *came* death, by man *came* also the resurrection of the dead. For as in Adam all die, even so in Christ shall all be made alive" (1 Cor. 15:20–22 KJV).

Paul calls Jesus's resurrection the "firstfruits of them that slept." If there is a first fruit, this indicates that there should be second, third, and so on. I want you to notice that Paul goes back to Adam and how everything changed with Adam's sin. He says the same thing will happen with Jesus's obedience. All were made in the likeness of death at the fall of Adam, but all will be made alive in Christ. In other words, all who are in Christ will be raised bodily from the dead. I want you to remember that Paul used the fall of Adam as a type and shadow of the resurrection, because that will mean something to us a little later.

"But some *man* will say how are the dead raised up? And with what body do they come? *Thou fool*, that which thou sowest is not quickened, except it die: And that which thou sowest, thou sowest not that body that shall be, but bare grain, it may chance of wheat, or of some other *grain*: But God giveth it a body as it hath pleased him, and to every seed his own body. All flesh *is* not the same flesh: but *there is* one *kind of* flesh of men, another flesh of beasts, another of fishes, *and* another of birds. *There are* also celestial bodies, and bodies terrestrial: but the glory of the celestial *is* one, and the *glory* of the terrestrial *is* another. *There is* one glory of the sun, and another glory of the moon, and another glory of the stars: for *one* star differeth from *another* star in glory. So also *is* the resurrection of the dead. It is sown in corruption; it is raised in incorruption: It is sown in dishonour; it is raised in glory: it is sown in weakness; it is raised in power: It is sown a natural body; it is raised a spiritual body. There is a natural body, and there is a spiritual body. And so it is written, The first man Adam was made a living soul; the last Adam *was made* a quickening spirit. Howbeit that *was* not first which is spiritual, but that which is natural; and afterward that which is

93

spiritual. The first man *is* of the earth, earthy: the second man *is* the Lord from heaven. As *is* the earthy, such *are* they also that are earthy: and as *is* the heavenly, such *are* they also that are heavenly. And as we have borne the image of the earthy, we shall also bear the image of the heavenly. Now this I say, brethren, that flesh and blood cannot inherit the kingdom of God; neither doth corruption inherit incorruption.

Behold, I shew you a mystery; We shall not all sleep, but we shall all be changed, In a moment, in the twinkling of an eye, at the last trump: for the trumpet shall sound, and the dead shall be raised incorruptible, and we shall be changed" (1 Cor. 15:35–52 KJV).

Paul is leading up to this point. This resurrection will be a bodily resurrection and the resurrected bodies will be like Jesus's body. The resurrection is what we call the rapture. Again, in the first letter to the Thessalonians, Paul writes:

"But I would not have you to be ignorant, brethren, concerning them which are asleep, that ye sorrow not, even as others which have no hope. For if we believe that Jesus died and rose again, even so them also which sleep in Jesus will God bring with him. For this we say unto you by the word of the Lord, that we which are alive *and* remain unto the coming of the Lord shall not prevent them which are asleep. For the Lord himself shall descend from heaven with a shout, with the voice of the archangel, *and with the trump of God: and the dead in Christ shall rise first: Then we which are alive and remain shall be caught up together with them in the clouds*, to meet the Lord in the air: and so shall we ever be with the Lord. Wherefore comfort one another with these words" (1 Thess. 4:13–18 KJV, emphasis mine).

Paul does not call it "the rapture." This term is one that modern prophecy teachers have coined. The words "caught up" have, as one definition, the word "rapture." It doesn't matter what you call it. It is the resurrection of our physical bodies, being changed to be like Jesus's body.

Now that we know what the rapture is, let's find out what happens during the rapture. In Romans 8, Paul contrasts the Spirit with the flesh, and he makes some important statements that will help us.

"And if Christ *be* in you, the body *is* dead because of sin; but the Spirit *is* life because of righteousness" (Romans 8:10 KJV).

Paul states that if Christ is in you, your body is dead because of sin, but your spirit lives because of the righteousness of Christ in you. Your physical body is dead! It is mortal because it does not have the life of Christ like your Spirit does. Read what Paul writes next:

"But if the Spirit of him that raised up Jesus from the dead dwell in you, he that raised up Christ from the dead shall also *quicken* your mortal bodies by his Spirit that dwelleth in you" (Romans 8:11 KJV, emphasis mine).

If the Spirit of him that raised up Jesus from the dead dwell in you, he will make your mortal body alive! The Holy Spirit will raise your physical body from the dead.

"Therefore, brethren, we are debtors, not to the flesh, to live after the flesh. For if ye live after the flesh, ye shall die: but if ye through the Spirit do mortify the deeds of the body, ye shall live. For as many as are led by the Spirit of God, they are the sons of God. For ye have not received the spirit of bondage again to fear; but ye have received the Spirit of adoption, whereby we cry, Abba, Father. The Spirit itself beareth witness with our spirit, that we are the children of God: *And if children, then heirs; heirs of God, and joint-heirs with Christ; if so be that we suffer with him, that we may be also glorified together. For I reckon that the sufferings of this present time are not worthy to be compared with the glory which shall be revealed in us*" (Romans 8:12–18 KJV, emphasis mine).

If we suffer with Jesus, we shall also be glorified together with him. The Holy Spirit within us will glorify or resurrect our mortal bodies at the time of the rapture. The Apostle Paul mentions our resurrection twice. The next verse is absolutely critical to understanding what Paul is trying to say.

"For the earnest expectation of the creature waiteth for the manifestation of the sons of God" (Romans 8:19 KJV).

This Scripture is saying that creation is waiting for the manifestation of the sons of God. We can ask two questions. What is the manifestation of the sons of God, and why is creation waiting for this event? Remember, context is critical. Let's look at the following Scriptures to answer these two questions.

"For the earnest expectation of the creature waiteth for the manifestation of the sons of God. For the creature was made subject to vanity, not willingly, but by reason of him who hath subjected *the same* in hope, Because the creature itself also shall be delivered from the bondage of corruption into the glorious liberty of the children of God. For we know that the whole creation groaneth and travaileth in pain together until now. And not only *they*, but ourselves also, which have the firstfruits of the Spirit, even we ourselves groan within ourselves, waiting for the adoption, *to wit*, the redemption of our body" (Romans 8:19–23 KJV).

Creation is waiting for something, but did you notice that we are also waiting? We are waiting for the adoption, the redemption or resurrection of our body. The manifestation of the sons of God is the redemption of our physical body. We know this because both we and creation are waiting for the same thing, the redemption of our body. Now why is creation waiting for the rapture to occur? We are going to be changed, our bodies will be made immortal, and there will be no curse or death. What does that have to do with creation? Verse 20 says that creation was made subject to vanity or sin, not willingly, but by reason of him (Adam) who subjected the same in hope. Adam subjected all of creation to the curse of death when he sinned. You will understand why that is relevant in just a moment. Verse 21 says that creation itself *also* shall be delivered from the bondage of corruption (the curse Adam placed on the earth) into the glorious liberty of the children of God. In other words, creation will enter into the same liberty that we enter when we are resurrected. When? Creation is waiting for the rapture because it will be delivered to it at the same time as it is given to us! The curse will be removed from the earth when the rapture occurs. That's in the context of these Scriptures. This will help you to see more clearly. Verse 20 is the reason why creation was under the curse. Notice how it reads from verse 19 to verse 21.

"For the earnest expectation of the creature waiteth for the manifestation of the sons of God."

"Because the creature itself also shall be delivered from the bondage of corruption into the glorious liberty of the children of God" (Romans 8:19, 21 KJV).

This is pretty clear. The curse will be removed from creation when the rapture occurs.

Now let's follow the rules of interpretation. The type and shadow of the rapture is found in Genesis. In fact, Paul mentioned it in both of the Scriptures we have read—it is the Fall of Adam. God gave Adam complete dominion over all of creation.

"O LORD our Lord, how excellent *is* thy name in all the earth! who hast set thy glory above the heavens. Out of the mouth of babes and sucklings hast thou ordained strength because of thine enemies, that thou mightest still the enemy and the avenger.

When I consider thy heavens, the work of thy fingers, the moon and the stars, which thou hast ordained; What is man, that thou art mindful of him? and the son of man, that thou visitest him? For thou hast made him a little lower than the angels, and hast crowned him with glory and honour. *Thou madest him to have dominion over the works of thy hands; thou hast put all things under his feet:* All sheep and oxen, yea, and the beasts of the field; The fowl of the air, and the fish of the sea, *and whatsoever* passeth through the paths of the seas. O LORD our Lord, how excellent *is* thy name in all the earth!" (Psalms 8:1–9 KJV, emphasis mine).

God placed all things under Adam's feet, according to Psalms 8:6, and when Adam sinned, everything under his authority was affected.

"And unto Adam he said, Because thou hast hearkened unto the voice of thy wife, and hast eaten of the tree, of which I commanded thee, saying, Thou shalt not eat of it: *cursed is the ground for thy sake*; in sorrow shalt thou eat *of* it all the days of thy life; Thorns also and thistles shall it bring forth to thee; and thou shalt eat the herb of the field; In the sweat of thy face shalt thou eat bread, till thou return unto the ground; for out of it wast thou taken: for dust thou *art*, and unto dust shalt thou return" (Gen. 3:17–19 KJV, emphasis mine).

This is important because our body is made of the same earth that was cursed that day. Adam no longer has that authority, because Jesus said "all authority has been given to him." When the rapture occurs and the body of Christ is raised from the dead, everything under Jesus's authority has to follow, just like it did when Adam sinned. All of creation followed Adam into sin, but when Jesus's body (believers) is raised from the dead, all of creation will follow us into the glorious liberty of the children of God. This is echoed by Paul.

"For since by man *came* death, by man *came* also the resurrection of the dead. For as in Adam all die, even so in Christ shall all be made alive" (1 Cor. 15:21–22 KJV).

There is the type and shadow. Let's confirm this further with more Scripture.

"For our conversation is in heaven; from whence also we look for the Saviour, the Lord Jesus Christ: Who shall change our vile body, that it may be fashioned like unto his glorious body, according to the working whereby he is able even to subdue all things unto himself" (Phil. 3:20–21 KJV).

We look for Jesus, who will change our vile body, that it may be fashioned like his glorious body. That is the rapture. Correct? Look what happens when Jesus changes our body. He is able to subdue ALL THINGS UNTO HIMSELF. The resurrection of our bodies is the tool that Jesus uses to subdue everything else! This Scripture literally says that the changing or resurrection of our body enables Jesus to subdue all things unto himself. This is another way of saying that when the rapture takes place, the curse on the earth will be removed. We have found two Scriptures and a type and shadow to confirm this interpretation. Now let's go back to where we started and see if we can find this same pattern in those Scriptures. Remember the famous Scripture that is used so often during discussions of the rapture?

"In a moment, in the twinkling of an eye, at the last trump: for the trumpet shall sound, and the dead shall be raised incorruptible, and we shall be changed" (1 Cor. 15:51–52 KJV).

Let's read on and find the result of this change.

"For this corruptible must put on incorruption, and this mortal *must* put on immortality. So when this corruptible shall have put on incorruption, and this mortal shall have put on immortality, then shall be brought to pass the saying that is written, Death is swallowed up in victory. O death, where *is* thy sting? O grave, where *is* thy victory?" (1 Cor. 15:53–55 KJV).

He says, when the rapture occurs, *Death* will be swallowed up in victory. Did you get that? *Death* itself will be consumed by complete victory. If death itself is eliminated, how can there be a curse on the earth? "O *grave*, where is thy victory?" Our physical, made-of-dirt bodies will be raised from the dead, and all the other dirt on the earth will be released from the bondage that Adam created in the beginning! That revelation was hidden right there in this verse the whole time.

Before we move on, I want to present a principle, introduced by Paul, which is crucial to our understanding of the next Scriptures.

"Knowing that he which raised up the Lord Jesus shall raise up us also by Jesus, and shall present *us* with you. For all things *are* for your sakes, that the abundant grace might through the thanksgiving of many redound to the glory of God. For which cause we faint not; but though our outward man perish, yet the inward *man* is renewed day by day. For our light affliction, which is but for a moment, worketh for us a far more exceeding *and* eternal weight of glory; While we look not at the things which are seen, but at the things which are not seen: for the things which are seen *are* temporal; but the things which are not seen *are* eternal" (2 Cor. 4:14–18 KJV).

Paul says the things that are seen are temporary and the things we cannot see are eternal. Things that are eternal never change. They cannot be moved in any way. Temporary things change. The kingdom of God is eternal, so it will never change or be moved. That's why we can hold on to the firm foundation of the eternal Word of God. Sin is temporary. The curse upon creation is temporary, and can be moved. Now, from this perspective, let's move on to the book of Hebrews.

"For ye are not come unto the mount that might be touched, and that burned with fire, nor unto blackness, and darkness, and tempest, And the sound of a trumpet, and the voice of words; which *voice* they that heard intreated that the word should not be spoken to them any more: (For they could not endure that which was commanded, And if so much as a beast touch the mountain, it shall be stoned, or thrust through with a dart: And so terrible was the sight, *that* Moses said, I exceedingly fear and quake)" (Heb. 12:18–21 KJV).

The mount referenced here is Mount Sinai, where the law was given to the children of Israel. This is a picture of God coming in judgment. The law represents judgment because if the law was not kept, all that was left was wrath. God came down in fire on Mount Sinai—what a sight it must have been. While Moses was away on the mountain, the children of Israel were worshipping another god (the golden calf). I could go into another type and shadow here that shows the judgment on Israel again, but I will let you study that on your own. The point here is that we are not called to Mount Sinai, which is the law. What are we being called to?

"But ye are come unto mount Sion, and unto the city of the living God, the heavenly Jerusalem, and to an innumerable company of angels" (Heb. 12:22 KJV).

We are called to Mount Zion, the mount where the sacrifice of Jesus was made, and unto the heavenly Jerusalem. Notice that the first mountain is earthly and the second is heavenly. The first is temporary and the second is eternal.

"To the general assembly and church of the firstborn, which are written in heaven, and to God the Judge of all, and to the spirits of just men made perfect, And to Jesus the mediator of the new covenant, and to the blood of sprinkling, that speaketh better things than *that of* Abel. See that ye refuse not him that speaketh. For if they escaped not who refused him that spake on earth, much more *shall not* we *escape*, if we turn away from him that *speaketh* from heaven: Whose voice then shook the earth: but now he hath promised, saying, Yet once more I shake not the earth only, but also heaven" (Heb. 12:23–26 KJV).

God's voice shook the earth when he spoke at Mount Sinai, and he promises a second shaking of earth and heaven. The introduction of the law shook the earth because it was through this law, which Jesus kept, that he was able to make a way for us and defeat Satan. What is the second shaking?

"And this *word*, Yet once more, signifieth the removing of those things that are shaken, as of things that are made, that those things which cannot be shaken may remain" (Heb. 12:27 KJV).

This second shaking is the removal of all the things that can be shaken. Everything temporary will be removed from earth and heaven at the time of this shaking. He gives us the reason why here as well. The temporary things (sin and the curse on the earth) are removed so that the things which cannot be moved (or are eternal) may remain. We have already studied how the rapture is the vehicle that God will use to remove the curse from the earth. This is also what he is talking about here. Do you remember that Death will be swallowed up in victory? How will this happen?

"Wherefore we receiving a kingdom which cannot be moved, let us have grace, whereby we may serve God acceptably with reverence and godly fear: *For our God is a consuming fire*" (Heb. 12:28–29 KJV, emphasis mine).

God will consume or swallow in victory all things that are not of him. Do you remember how Jesus is going to return?

"And to you who are troubled rest with us, when the Lord Jesus shall be revealed from heaven with his mighty angels, *In flaming fire* taking vengeance on them that know not God, and that obey not the gospel of our Lord Jesus Christ: Who shall be punished with everlasting destruction from the presence of the Lord, and from the glory of his power; When he shall come to be glorified in his saints, and to be admired in all them that believe (because our testimony among you was believed) in that day" (2 Thess. 1:7–10 KJV, emphasis mine).

Jesus is coming back in flaming fire! When Jesus comes back in flames, we will meet him in the air and our bodies will be instantly changed into the same flaming fire. Every Christian from around the world will rise up in the air in a flame of fire. And around the earth, the curse will be instantly removed from the earth. Verse 10 says that Jesus is coming to be GLORIFIED in his saints. The fire of Jesus will shake the heavens and the earth and remove all things that can be shaken, leaving behind all things that cannot be shaken. This is the rapture of the Church of Jesus Christ. Hebrews 12:26–27 comes from the book of Haggai. The context of the book of Haggai is that Jerusalem and the temple had been destroyed and the Jews had come back to Israel from Babylon. They were trying to rebuild Jerusalem and the temple again.

"In the seventh *month*, in the one and twentieth *day* of the month, came the word of the LORD by the prophet Haggai, saying, Speak now to Zerubbabel the son of Shealtiel, governor of Judah, and to Joshua the son of Josedech, the high priest, and to the residue of the people, saying, Who *is* left among you that saw this house in her first glory?

and how do ye see it now? *is it* not in your eyes in comparison of it as nothing?" (Hag. 2:1–3 KJV).

When "this house" is mentioned, it is referring to the temple in Jerusalem. They were rebuilding the temple during "troublesome times," exactly as the book of Daniel said they would (see Daniel 9:25).

"Yet now be strong, O Zerubbabel, saith the LORD; and be strong, O Joshua, son of Josedech, the high priest; and be strong, all ye people of the land, saith the LORD, and work: for I *am* with you, saith the LORD of hosts: *According to* the word that I covenanted with you when ye came out of Egypt, so my spirit remaineth among you: fear ye not. For thus saith the LORD of hosts; Yet once, it *is* a little while, and I will shake the heavens, and the earth, and the sea, and the dry *land*; And I will shake all nations, and the desire of all nations shall come: and I will fill this house with glory, saith the LORD of hosts" (Hag. 2:4–7 KJV).

God is saying to them at that time that the temple would be completed and he would fill that house (the temple) with glory. The appearance of the second temple would be even more glorious than the first.

The writer of Hebrews uses this as a type and shadow of the removal of the things that can be moved (sin and the curse). In this context, the house is the whole of creation, and through these verses, God is saying that he will fill the whole of creation with his glory! Sin and the curse are darkness, and the glory of God is the light. When a light is turned on, where does the darkness go? It vanishes! This fits exactly with the rapture of the church. We will receive GLORIFIED bodies! What an awesome event that will be!

I don't know if you realized it, but this means that the second coming of Christ and the rapture of the church must happen simultaneously—they are the same event. The changing of our bodies will be the fire that takes vengeance on God's enemies, destroying their physical bodies through glory of our God upon Jesus and ourselves. It is this fire that consumes all things that are not of God and that brings the new heaven and new earth into reality. Peter writes:

"For this they willingly are ignorant of, that by the word of God the heavens were of old, and the earth standing out of the water and in the water: Whereby the world that then was, being overflowed with water, perished: But the heavens and the earth, which are now, by the same word are kept in store, reserved unto *fire* against the day of judgment and perdition of ungodly men" (2 Peter 3:5–7 KJV, emphasis mine).

The heavens and the earth are reserved unto fire. What fire is this? It is the glory of God upon Jesus and the church when we are raptured.

"But the day of the Lord will come as a thief in the night; in which the heavens shall pass away with a great noise, and the elements shall melt *with fervent heat*, the earth also and the works that are therein shall be burned up.

Seeing then *that* all these things shall be dissolved, what manner *of persons* ought ye to be in *all* holy conversation and godliness, Looking for and hasting unto the coming of the day of God, wherein the heavens being on fire shall be dissolved, and the elements shall melt with fervent heat? Nevertheless we, according to his promise, look for new heavens and a new earth, wherein dwelleth righteousness" (2 Peter 3:10–13 KJV, emphasis mine).

The new heavens and new earth are manifested at the second coming of Jesus and the rapture of the church. This is pretty clear. Did you see that verse 10 said the works are burned up as well? This gives us some insight into another Scripture.

"For other foundation can no man lay than that is laid, which is Jesus Christ. Now if any man build upon this foundation gold, silver, precious stones, wood, hay, stubble" (1 Cor. 3:11–12 KJV).

Paul is teaching about carnal Christians and how they should lay the right works on the foundation of Jesus Christ. Notice how there are two groups of foundations—gold, silver, and precious stones and wood, hay, and stubble. The first group are not burned or destroyed by fire, but the second group is completely consumed. These are two kinds of "works" we can do on the earth.

"Every man's work shall be made manifest: for the day shall declare it, because it shall be revealed by fire; and the fire shall try every man's work of what sort it is" (1 Cor. 3:13 KJV).

The works will be revealed by fire. Which fire? It's the same fire that creates the new heaven and new earth. The works are revealed as Godly or evil, and the evil works will be removed. That's how we know what kind of work it is. If it remains, it was a good and Godly work.

"If any man's work abide which he hath built thereupon, he shall receive a reward. If any man's work shall be burned, he shall suffer loss: but he himself shall be saved; yet so as by fire" (1 Cor. 3:14–15 KJV).

The last part of verse 15 says that the carnal Christian will suffer loss because of evil works, but he himself will be saved BY THE FIRE. It makes sense that the fire saves him because he is being raised bodily from the dead during the rapture of the church, but he will not be rewarded for his carnal, dead works.

In summary, the rapture is the last thing that happens because death is removed from the earth and a new heaven and earth are created at the same time as Jesus's second coming to the earth. The wicked will be instantly judged by the fire and glory of Jesus and the Church. The rewards will be determined at that time as well. Our God is a consuming fire!

Chapter 10

—————— 10 ——————

OUR PROPHETIC FUTURE

HOPEFULLY, YOU HAVE STUDIED AND prayed concerning the things you have read previously in this book. The ideas that have been shared, no doubt, have changed your perspective on Scripture. I recommend you read through your Bible with this new perspective, expecting God to reveal more things to you. There is much more to be learned. There are so many more revelations to discover, but you have to be in the right position to receive them. When God leads you into truth through the Holy Spirit, he puts you in position for revelation of his word. God wants to reveal to you everything you can handle. I want you to understand this principle perfectly. God is no respecter of persons. What do I mean? Don't think that I am some great and perfect preacher. I am just a man from a small town who dared to seek God's answers for the things he did not understand. I am a nobody, yet God answered my call. It does not matter who you are or where you come from, God will reveal himself to you. God wants to reveal himself more than you know. Dare to seek God and to believe in him! Dare to give him your all! God will take you places you have never dreamed of. He will show you revelations that the men and women of the Old Testament could not receive.

If we want to understand our prophetic future, we must understand the one principle that permeates the whole of Scripture. Faith! The whole Bible is a book of faith. Faith is the most important thing! You cannot be saved without it, and it's impossible to please God without faith. Faith is the victory that overcomes the world. What is faith in its simplest form? It is the ability to believe. If you don't have faith, you don't believe. Let's look into what Jesus had to say about faith.

"And on the morrow, when they were come from Bethany, he was hungry: And seeing a fig tree afar off having leaves, he came, if haply he might find any thing thereon: and when he came to it, he found nothing but leaves; for the time of figs was not *yet*. And Jesus answered and said unto it, No man eat fruit of thee hereafter for ever. And his disciples heard *it*" (Mark 11:12–14 KJV).

This is just a side note, but the action of Jesus in cursing the fig tree is prophetic of Israel being cursed for not producing the fruit God expected of them.

"And they come to Jerusalem: and Jesus went into the temple, and began to cast out them that sold and bought in the temple, and overthrew the tables of the moneychangers, and the seats of them that sold doves; And would not suffer that any man should carry any vessel through the temple. And he taught, saying unto them, Is it not written, My house shall be called of all nations the house of prayer? but ye have made it a den of thieves. And the scribes and chief priests heard it, and sought how they might destroy him: for they feared him, because all the people was astonished at his doctrine. And when even was come, he went out of the city. And in the morning, as they passed by, they saw the fig tree dried up from the roots. And Peter calling to remembrance saith unto him, Master, behold, the fig tree which thou cursedst is withered away" (Mark 11:15–21 KJV).

The fig tree that Jesus cursed was dried up when they returned back to it. Peter pointed it out to Jesus, and here is how Jesus responded.

"And Jesus answering saith unto them, Have faith in God. For verily I say unto you, That whosoever shall say unto this mountain, Be thou removed, and be thou cast into the sea; and shall not doubt in his heart, but shall believe that those things which he saith shall come to pass; he shall have whatsoever he saith" (Mark 11:22–23 KJV).

Jesus just explained how to have faith. He begins by saying "verily," which means truly. Think about this: Jesus, the Messiah, the Christ, is saying, I'm telling you the truth. This must mean that what Jesus is about to say is a hard truth to comprehend. Jesus also includes who this truth applies to, "whosoever." Whosoever means you and me and everyone else. Whosoever shall say unto this mountain, you be removed and be cast into the sea and not doubt, but BELIEVE, you will have WHATSOEVER you say. This is tremendous! If you say something and believe it will happen, IT WILL HAPPEN! If you are thinking right now that you don't believe that, what do you think will happen if you say something and don't believe it will come to pass? Then, it won't happen. It's as simple as that. I also want to point out that this is something that was said, rather than prayed about to God. This is faith that you can speak the words and God will bring them to pass. So, how do we have faith in God? We speak things that agree with God's word and God's nature, and believe that those things will come to pass and we will have what we say. Jesus continues in the next verse, showing how faith works in prayer.

"Therefore I say unto you, What things soever ye desire, when ye pray, believe that ye receive *them*, and ye shall have *them*" (Mark 11:24 KJV).

Faith in your prayers works in this way: ask what you desire, believe that God will give it to you, and you shall receive it. That is why many people who pray, "Heavenly Father grant me such and such, IF IT BE THY WILL," don't always receive this from God. "If" is a word of doubt. Faith says God WILL give it to you. Faith is the belief that God will provide, and faith means knowing the WILL of God before you ask. Let me give you an example that will help. Let's say that you are leading a man in prayer to receive Jesus as his Savior. You go through the sinner's prayer with him, and he prays after you, confessing Jesus as his Lord. Afterward, you are excited about praying with this person to receive Jesus, but shortly after the prayer, he says, "I hope God saves me." You ask, what do you mean? Then, he quotes a Scripture to you.

"For my thoughts are not your thoughts, neither are your ways my ways, saith the LORD. For as the heavens are higher than the earth, so are my ways higher than your ways, and my thoughts than your thoughts" (Isaiah 55:7–9 KJV).

Then, this person says that no one can know God's will because his thoughts are above our thoughts. What has that got to do with anything, you ask. He answers, no one can know whether they are saved because only God knows that. Wait a minute, you say, you don't know if it is God's will for you to be saved? No, he says, only God knows that. It's up to God whether or not he chooses us.

This person is still wondering whether God wants him to be saved. Is that person saved? No, because he does not believe or he doubts God's will to save him. Can you hope your way into heaven? Of course not. You must believe, without a doubt, that it is God's will for you to be saved and confess (or say) that he is Lord, believing that you will receive him, and then you are saved. In order to have faith, you MUST know the will of God first. A person who doesn't know the will of God concerning their salvation cannot be saved until they BELIEVE it is God's will for them to be saved. Faith knows the will of God!

This same principle applies to all areas of faith. For instance, is it God's will to heal the sick? If you don't believe it is God's will, you will not be able to receive divine healing from him. Why? There is doubt. Jesus said, "believe and doubt not in your heart." If you don't believe, you have doubt. In order to receive healing, you must KNOW that it is God's will for you to be healed or you won't receive healing.

This is the struggle that Israel experienced. They did not understand righteousness by faith, and there is no other way to gain righteousness before God except through faith in Jesus Christ. Israel struggled with the law, believing that keeping it made them righteous. However, this was a dividing line. Some found faith through Jesus and knew and understood the will of God. Others, who continued to follow the law, were blind to the will of God. God knew this would happen and used their lack of faith to advance the gospel to the whole world. Faith is the main principle of the whole Bible; understanding the Word of God and faith go hand in hand.

Now, on our journey through our prophetic future, we have to understand that the kingdom of God was removed from Israel and given to the Gentiles because Israel, as a whole, lacked faith in Jesus the Messiah. Is God finished with Israel? Let's find out what Jesus said on this subject.

"There were present at that season some that told him of the Galilaeans, whose blood Pilate had mingled with their sacrifices. And Jesus answering said unto them, Suppose ye that these Galilaeans were sinners above all the Galilaeans, because they suffered such things? I tell you, Nay: but, except ye repent, ye shall all likewise perish. Or those eighteen, upon whom the tower in Siloam fell, and slew them, think ye that they were sinners above all men that dwelt in Jerusalem? I tell you, Nay: but, except ye repent, ye shall all likewise perish" (Luke 13:1–5 KJV).

Jesus is referring to the destruction of Jerusalem here. If they did not repent or turn from their beliefs, they also would be killed. Afterward, Jesus illustrated his meaning with a parable.

"He spake also this parable; A certain *man* had a fig tree planted in his vineyard; and he came and sought fruit thereon, and found none. Then said he unto the dresser of his vineyard, Behold, these three years I come seeking fruit on this fig tree, and find none: cut it down; why cumbereth it the ground? And he answering said unto him, Lord, let it alone this year also, till I shall dig about it, and dung *it*: And if it bear fruit, *well*: and if not, *then* after that thou shalt cut it down" (Luke 13:6–9 KJV).

The fig tree represents Israel, and the fruit from the fig tree is faith in the Messiah. Jesus didn't find fruit on the tree of Israel. What did he say would happen? After a short time, Israel would be cut down like a tree that didn't bear any fruit. However, Jesus didn't stop there. Let's continue on and see what he says.

"Then said one unto him, Lord, are there few that be saved? And he said unto them, Strive to enter in at the strait gate: for many, I say unto you, will seek to enter in, and shall not be able" (Luke 13:23–24 KJV).

Someone asks Jesus if just a few will be saved, and Jesus essentially answers, yes. He also said there would be some who would try to enter in the kingdom of God, but would not be able. We will come back to this a little later. There is a major point here that we can glean. Jesus tells another parable to explain it.

"When once the master of the house is risen up, and hath shut to the door, and ye begin to stand without, and to knock at the door, saying, Lord, Lord, open unto us; and he shall answer and say unto you, I know you not whence ye are: Then shall ye begin to say, We have eaten and drunk in thy presence, and thou hast taught in our streets. But he shall say, I tell you, I know you not whence ye are; depart from me, all *ye* workers of iniquity. There shall be weeping and gnashing of teeth, when ye shall see Abraham, and Isaac, and Jacob, and all the prophets, in the kingdom of God, and you yourselves thrust out. And they shall come from the east, and from the west, and from the north, and from the south, and shall sit down in the kingdom of God. And, behold, there are last which shall be first, and there are first which shall be last" (Luke 13:25–30 KJV).

Jesus is the master of the house. He shows the people's reaction when they finally realize that Jesus is their Messiah, but this realization would come too late to save them. The door of the Gospel would be closed to the Jews. They would eventually realize that Jesus had taught in their streets and they had eaten and drank in his presence, but Jesus would call them "workers of iniquity" and force them to depart from his presence. They would even see Abraham, Isaac, Jacob, and all the prophets in the kingdom of God, but they would be thrust out. This sounds just like the parable of the ten virgins (Matt. 25) in which Jesus says that not only would the Jews be thrust out, but people from the south, east, west, north, and south (Gentiles) would sit down in the kingdom of God. The last statement Jesus makes here is the most important. "There are last which shall be first, and there are first which shall be last." What does this mean? Jesus was sent FIRST to the house of Israel, where the Jews were the first to hear the Gospel. Jesus said the first (Israel) would become last and the last (Gentiles) would become first. This means that the gospel would go to the Gentiles, and they would receive it instead of rejecting it. In the same manner that Jesus exclusively preached to the Jewish people, the Gospel would be preached to the Gentiles until the fullness of the Gentiles are come in (Romans 11:25). This means that Israel will receive, instead of rejecting the Gospel, but they will be last to do so. God is not finished with Israel. Israel will be the last nation on the earth to receive Jesus as their Messiah, and when they do, this is a sign of the second coming of Christ. If you are looking for a sign of the times, that is it. Before that can happen, though, the Gentiles must first come into the kingdom of God. There is a lot of work to do.

With that said, don't think that God has completely forsaken Israel, as some have said. They will enter into the kingdom of God, but they will be last. If you read Romans 9, 10, and 11, you will see that this is the subject on which the Apostle Paul is writing. He shows how Israel will come into the kingdom of God.

"I say then, Hath God cast away his people? God forbid. For I also am an Israelite, of the seed of Abraham, *of* the tribe of Benjamin. God hath not cast away his people which he foreknew. Wot ye not what the Scripture saith of Elias? how he maketh intercession to God against Israel, saying, Lord, they have killed thy prophets, and digged down thine altars; and I am left alone, and they seek my life. But what saith the answer of God unto him? I have reserved to myself seven thousand men, who have not bowed the knee to *the image of* Baal. Even so then at this present time also there is a remnant according to the election of grace" (Romans 11:1–5 KJV).

Paul proclaims that God has NOT cast his people away. He shows, by the type and shadow of Elijah, how a remnant would be saved in Israel during the time in which Paul was living. Please study your Bible in light of these types and shadows. This is how Paul understood the things that he did.

"And if by grace, then *is it* no more of works: otherwise grace is no more grace. But if *it be* of works, then is it no more grace: otherwise work is no more work. What then? Israel hath not obtained that which he seeketh for; but the election hath obtained it, and the rest were blinded (According as it is written, God hath given them the spirit of slumber, eyes that they should not see, and ears that they should not hear;) unto this day. And David saith, Let their table be made a snare, and a trap, and a stumbling block, and a recompence unto them: Let their eyes be darkened, that they may not see, and bow down their back alway" (Romans 11:6–10 KJV).

Paul shows God's plan in what happened to Israel, and then he says that the fall of Israel was the saving of the Gentiles and that the Gentiles would make the Jews jealous. Remember that, we will elaborate on this point.

"I say then, Have they stumbled that they should fall? God forbid: but *rather* through their fall salvation *is come* unto the Gentiles, for to provoke them to jealousy. Now if the fall of them *be* the riches of the world, and the diminishing of them the riches of the Gentiles; how much more their fulness? For I speak to you Gentiles, inasmuch as I am the apostle of the Gentiles, I magnify mine office: If by any means I may provoke to emulation *them which are* my flesh, and might save some of them. For if the casting away of them *be* the reconciling of the world, what *shall* the receiving *of them be*, but life from the dead?" (Romans 11:11–15 KJV).

Wow! What a powerful statement! If the casting away of Israel is the reconciling of the world, what could the receiving of them be except life from the dead? Paul is saying that when Israel receives the kingdom of God and Jesus as Messiah, the rapture will take place!

"For if the firstfruit *be* holy, the lump *is* also *holy*: and if the root *be* holy, so *are* the branches. And if some of the branches be broken off, and thou, being a wild olive tree, wert graffed in among them, and with them partakest of the root and fatness of the olive tree; Boast not against the branches. But if thou boast, thou bearest not the root, but the root thee. Thou wilt say then, The branches were broken off, that I might be graffed in. Well; because of unbelief they were broken off, and thou standest by faith. Be not highminded, but fear: For if God spared not the natural branches, *take heed* lest he also spare not thee. Behold therefore the goodness and severity of God: on them which fell, severity; but toward thee, goodness, if thou continue in *his* goodness: otherwise thou also shalt be cut off. And they also, if they abide not still in unbelief, shall be graffed in: *for God is able to graff them in again*. For if thou wert cut out of the olive tree which is wild by nature, and wert graffed contrary to nature into a good olive tree: how much more shall these, which be the natural *branches*, be graffed into their own olive tree? For I would not, brethren, that ye should be ignorant of this mystery, lest ye should be wise in your own conceits; that blindness in part is happened to Israel, *until the fulness of the Gentiles be come in*. And so all Israel shall be saved: as it is written, There shall come out of Sion the Deliverer, and shall turn away ungodliness from Jacob: For this *is* my covenant unto them, when I shall take away their sins. As concerning the gospel, *they are* enemies for your sakes: but as touching the election, *they are* beloved for the fathers' sakes" (Romans 11:16–28 KJV, emphasis mine).

We have established that Israel will receive Jesus and that they will be the last to do so. I just want to make an important point here. How many times have you heard a preacher say that only a few will be saved because the Bible says, "narrow is the gate and there be few that find it"? The implication is that only a few people are going to make it to heaven. That simply is not true. Jesus was referring only to the Jews at that time. He was speaking of the remnant or the few that would be saved during that time, not in our time.

"Then said one unto him, Lord, are there few that be saved? And he said unto them, Strive to enter in at the strait gate: for many, I say unto you, will seek to enter in, and shall not be able" (Luke 13:23–24 KJV).

The difference is that we are Gentiles, not part of the Jewish remnant. It was prophesied that only a few Israelites would be saved. There are no prophecies about the number of Gentiles who will be saved. We can't take that statement out of context and apply it to the Gentiles because it doesn't fit. Unless I have simply missed it, I have not seen any Scripture that limits the number of people saved among the Gentiles. In fact, it seems to me that when Paul says the "fullness" of the Gentiles comes in, he means…well, let's just say a lot. We cannot use this Scripture as an excuse because we are not receiving strong results from our presentation of the Gospel to the world. If what you are doing is not working, you should pray and ask God what you should be doing differently. We are supposed to bring forth the fruits of the Gospel, which primarily means bringing the lost into the kingdom of God. Don't make excuses for failure. Hone your skills as a fisher of men and be fruitful in your efforts to win people into the kingdom. This is the heart of God.

Paul suggests that we, the Gentile group who are now receiving the Gospel, are going to make the Jews jealous. What does he mean? It's very simple. We have what they should have received. When the body of Christ shows the fruits of the Gospel instead of a religion to the Jews, the Jews will become jealous and desire a relationship with God again. Let's dig further into this and see what it entails.

We are about to see something else that MUST occur before the second coming of Jesus. It's a big thing, and it explains where we are in the process of time.

"I therefore, the prisoner of the Lord, beseech you that ye walk worthy of the vocation wherewith ye are called,

With all lowliness and meekness, with longsuffering, forbearing one another in love; Endeavouring to keep the unity of the Spirit in the bond of peace. *There is* one body, and one Spirit, even as ye are called in one hope of your calling; One Lord, one faith, one baptism, One God and Father of all, who *is* above all, and through all, and in you all. But unto every one of us is given grace according to the measure of the gift of Christ. Wherefore he saith, When he ascended up on high, he led captivity captive, and gave gifts unto men. (Now that he ascended, what is it but that he also descended first into the lower parts of the earth? He that descended is the same also that ascended up far above all heavens, that he might fill all things.) And he gave some, apostles; and some, prophets; and some, evangelists; and some, pastors and teachers; For the perfecting of the saints, for the work of the ministry, for the edifying of the body of Christ: *Till* we all come in the unity of the faith, and of the knowledge of the Son of God, unto a perfect man, unto the measure of the stature of the fulness of Christ" (Eph. 4:1–13 KJV, emphasis mine).

Did you see that? One little word, "till." Paul said that we will have the fivefold ministry of apostles, prophets, pastors, evangelists, and teachers to build, strengthen, and teach us until we grow up! We are going to have to grow up before Jesus will return! What do I mean by grow up? The Scripture said, unto a perfect or mature man. We, the body of Christ, are going to have to become mature as a whole. How mature? We must look and act like Jesus Christ. Paul said we must grow unto the MEASURE OF THE STATURE OF THE FULNESS OF CHRIST. Some may think that just means getting saved, so let's make sure to interpret this correctly. Listen to what Paul says next.

"*That we henceforth be no more children, tossed to and fro, and carried about with every wind of doctrine,* by the sleight of men, *and* cunning craftiness, whereby they lie in wait to deceive; But speaking the truth in love, may grow up into him in all things, which is the head, *even* Christ" (Eph. 4:14–15 KJV, emphasis mine).

We must understand the doctrine correctly and not be led around by every slick-tongued preacher who appears. We must grow up in doctrine. Paul goes even further to say that we should grow up into him (Jesus) in ALL THINGS. How do you think a mature Christian would look? Jesus is our only true example of a mature person in Christ, because he is Christ. This means that in order for us to grow up into him in all things, we must do the things he did. We are his body, are we not? Then, we should be producing the same good fruit that Jesus did when he was on the earth.

From these Scriptures, we can see that we (the body of Christ) must grow into him in all things. Remember our rules of interpretation? We must have at least two witnesses to establish something as doctrine. Let me reiterate the point here. The fivefold ministry is not finished until the body of Christ grows up. We, the body of Christ, will heal the sick, cast out devils, perform miracles, and preach the gospel with power. That's what Jesus did, and he is our example. Let's look at our second Scripture.

"But now is Christ risen from the dead, and become the firstfruits of them that slept. For since by man came death, by man came also the resurrection of the dead. For as in Adam all die, even so in Christ shall all be made alive. But every man in his own order: Christ the firstfruits; afterward they that are Christ's at his coming" (1 Cor. 15:20–23 KJV).

Paul is preaching on the resurrection and how everyone in Christ will be raised up. We learned in the previous chapter that the resurrection or rapture will be the very last thing that takes place because it removes the curse from the earth at the same time. Paul is speaking of the order of the resurrection here, and basically says that we will be raised up during the second coming of Christ. Then will come the end of everything.

"Then cometh the end, when he shall have delivered up the kingdom to God, even the Father; when he shall have put down all rule and all authority and power. For he must reign, till he hath put all enemies under his feet" (1 Cor. 15:24–25 KJV).

At the resurrection, Jesus turns to the Father and delivers the kingdom over to him. I want you to notice something here. Verse 24 says that Jesus won't do that until he has removed all rulers, authorities, and powers that oppose him. That is very interesting, isn't it? Jesus must reign until…there's that word again. Jesus must reign until he has put all of his enemies under his feet. When does Jesus's reign start? It has to start before the rapture because of what is written in the next verse.

"The last enemy that shall be destroyed is death" (1 Cor. 15:26 KJV).

We have found that death is swallowed up in victory during the rapture, so the reign of Jesus must start before then. Is Jesus the king in the kingdom of God? Of course he is. When did he receive the kingdom? Jesus received the kingdom at his first coming.

"I saw in the night visions, and, behold, *one* like the Son of man came with the clouds of heaven, and came to the Ancient of days, and they brought him near before him. And there was given him dominion, and glory, *and a kingdom*, that all people, nations, and languages, should serve him: his dominion *is* an everlasting dominion, which shall not pass away, and his kingdom *that* which shall not be destroyed" (Dan. 7:13–14 KJV, emphasis mine).

Jesus also said:

"And when he was demanded of the Pharisees, when the kingdom of God should come, he answered them and said, The kingdom of God cometh not with observation: Neither shall they say, Lo here! or, lo there! for, behold, *the kingdom of God is within you*" (Luke 17:20–21 KJV, emphasis mine).

The kingdom Jesus received is a spiritual kingdom that resides on the inside of us. Jesus began to reign at the day of Pentecost when the Spirit was given, and he has been reigning since then. Paul said that Jesus will reign until ALL enemies will be put under his feet, meaning defeated. If Jesus has to put down all of his enemies (except death) before he can return, don't you think that all Jesus's enemies will have to be under our feet as well, since we are the BODY of Christ? Jesus prayed for us in John 17:20–23. Listen to his prayer for us.

"Neither pray I for these alone, but for them also which shall believe on me through their word; That they all may be one; as thou, Father, *art* in me, and I in thee, that *they also may be one in us*: that the world may believe that thou hast sent me. And the glory which thou gavest me I have given them; that they may be one, even as we are one: I in them, and thou in me, that they may be made perfect in one; and that the world may know that thou hast sent me, and hast loved them, as thou hast loved me" (John 17:20–23 KJV, emphasis mine).

If you are born again, you have become one with God in the spirit. Being one with Jesus, we must put all his enemies under our feet as well. What kind of enemies? Anything that pertains to the curse and to sin is an enemy of Jesus, including sickness, disease, and poverty, just to name a few. In other words, we have a responsibility to conquer the world through the love of God. We are supposed to win, not lose! People have a defeated mentality, thinking the worst is going to happen when the reality is that God is waiting on us to get up and obey him. When Jesus told the disciples to go into all the world and preach, he meant it.

"And he said unto them, Go ye into all the world, and preach the gospel to every creature. He that believeth and is baptized shall be saved; but he that believeth not shall be damned. *And these signs shall follow them that believe; In my name shall they cast out devils; they shall speak with new tongues; They shall take up serpents; and if they drink any deadly thing, it shall not hurt them; they shall lay hands on the sick, and they shall recover*" (Mark 16:15–18 KJV, emphasis mine).

All these things are meant for us today! Why should we pray for the sick to be healed? Sickness is an enemy of God. Why should we cast out devils? They're an enemy of God! Some may be thinking that this sort of thing passed away with the apostles. That cannot be true because Jesus said these signs will follow those that *believe*. Are you a believer? These signs should be following you. This is another way of saying that the body of Christ must grow up and mature. We have not fully done our job on the earth just yet.

Here is what will happen when we grow up. The Gentile believers will walk in the supernatural, as Jesus and the apostles did, and the Jews will take notice. Israel will become jealous of us because we have the God of Israel and the blessings that come with him. They will become hungry for God and accept Jesus as their Messiah, fulfilling the Scripture in Romans 11:11.

"I say then, Have they stumbled that they should fall? God forbid: but *rather* through their fall salvation *is come* unto the Gentiles, for to provoke them to jealousy" (Romans 11:10–11 KJV).

The kingdom of God will then be returned to the Jews.

There should be a revival from now until the rapture. We are supposed to defeat the devil. The Antichrist is not going take over the world and rule it for seven years. Jesus is ruling and reigning, and we should be reigning with him.

"For if by one man's offence death reigned by one; much more they which receive abundance of grace and of the gift of righteousness shall *reign in life* by one, Jesus Christ" (Romans 5:17 KJV, emphasis mine).

Jesus expects us to grow and do the things that he did.

"Believe me that I *am* in the Father, and the Father in me: or else believe me for the very works' sake" (John 14:10–11 KJV).

Basically, Jesus said to them, you can take my word for it or just believe because of the things I do. Healings, miracles, signs, and wonders are his works. Then, he puts the responsibility squarely on our shoulders.

"Verily, verily, I say unto you, *He that believeth on me, the works that I do shall he do also*; and greater *works* than these shall he do; because I go unto my Father. And whatsoever ye shall ask in my name, that will I do, that the Father may be glorified in the Son. If ye shall ask any thing in my name, I will do *it*" (John 14:12–14 KJV, emphasis mine).

If you believe in Jesus, then he expects you and me to do the same works he did. How are we going to do that? Everything done in Christ is through faith. You have to find out God's will, and have the faith to do these things. Let's grow up! Let's take responsibility! Study and pray for God's will, then go out and fulfill it! Start by studying your Scriptures.

I pray that this book have been a revelation that provokes you to go and do. I hope you have learned how to correctly study and interpret the Bible. Always confirm the revelations that God gives you, so you don't get off track. Let's go get 'em!

"The grace of our Lord Jesus Christ *be* with you all. Amen" (2 Thess. 3:18 KJV).

Epilogue

God is counting on you! The relationship that you have with God must be one of cooperation. God is relying on you and me to cooperate with him in order to accomplish his will on the earth. We are the body of Christ, and God is not going to do it without us. We are his hands, his feet, and his voice. We must grow up in Jesus in all things and do our job, which is seeking out and saving the lost. Every false doctrine holds us back from being effective for God in many different areas. Let's be diligent and destroy all of the false doctrines that fight against us and the Lord. I challenge you to listen to God, confirm your doctrines, and change the world through the power of the Word of God.

Your brother in Christ,
Kree Foster

Contact Information

Comments and questions are more than welcome. Whether you agree or disagree doesn't matter—I want to know what you think. Sometimes the best way to find the right answers is to ask the right questions.

Email:

jonkree@gmail.com

Website:

Israelandthelastdays.com